Preloved Chic

*Stylish Secrets to Elevate Your Wardrobe
With Second-Hand Fashion*

JENNIFER MELVILLE

OTHER BOOKS BY JENNIFER MELVILLE

Elevate the Everyday
Actions and Ideas to Enhance the Experience of Daily Life

Elevate Your Personal Style
Inspiration for the Everyday Woman

Elevate Your Health
*Inspiration and Motivation to Embrace and
Maintain a Healthy Lifestyle*

Elevate Your Life at Home
Inspiring Ideas to Add Joy, Peace and Magic to Your Homelife

Elevate Your Money Mindset
*Approach Your Finances With Positivity,
Confidence and Enthusiasm*

Seashells in my Pocket
50 Ways to Live a Beach Inspired Life

Paris in my Panties
Live Your Best (French Inspired) Life

Blissful Christmas
Glide Through the Holidays With Less Effort and More Joy

Cozy Up!
How to Thrive During the Coldest Months of the Year

Glow Up!
Sparkle at Any Age Inside and Out

CONTENTS

INTRODUCTION

Hello! Thank you so much for picking up this little book of mine. I'm so happy to have sparked your curiosity and interest in the wonderful world of second-hand fashion. Shopping the preloved clothing market is becoming more mainstream and accessible by the day. Consumers are quickly recognizing the countless benefits it has to offer, and it's time we all jumped on this bandwagon!

Whether we've crossed paths before, or this is your first time meeting me, I'd like to begin by introducing myself. I don't profess to be a fashionista! I consider myself to be an everyday woman (perhaps just like you?) I'm an accountant by trade, but more importantly, I'm a mother, wife, daughter, sister and friend. Over the last couple of decades, I've been exploring the concept of *elevating the everyday* in various areas of my life. The accountant in me loves approaching life with an analytical mind. I'm constantly tweaking my thoughts and behaviours in an effort to elevate my mindset, health, homelife, relationships, finances...and *style*!

Style may seem like a frivolous topic at first glance, but I've learned that it represents a form of personal expression that can have an enormous impact on our self-esteem and confidence. When you present yourself in a manner that feels pulled together and uplifted, your inner landscape starts to mirror your exterior.

As I embarked on a quest to elevate my personal style, I quickly realized that building a wardrobe with high-quality items made a lot of sense. Well-constructed pieces are more durable, and therefore can withstand the wear and tear life throws at them. I did, however, face one major roadblock—my *budget!* As a money-minded individual, I started to look for ways to stretch my fashion dollars as much as possible, which inevitably lead me to the land of preloved fashion.

When I was first introduced to the concept of building a wardrobe with second-hand finds, I immediately put up a wall. I wasn't convinced that as an everyday woman, I had the skills, knowledge or fashion sense to pull it off. (Can you relate to this sentiment?) I held the impression that second-hand success was reserved for resourceful fashionistas, skilled sleuths and lucky ducks (the types of people who seem to stumble upon dazzling treasures beneath a mountain of rags). Thank goodness I eventually opened my mind and set aside my insecurities and reservations. I quickly learned that second-hand shopping success is accessible to *all* of us!

I'm so excited to let you in on some of my most deliciously chic and stylish secrets. Shopping the preloved fashion scene is my *secret style weapon*! It allows me to fill my closet with high-quality, unique pieces that would normally fall outside my budget constraints. As an everyday woman, I have developed a set of shopping strategies that will help you procure a fabulously stylish wardrobe that is both budget-friendly and eco-conscious.

I do need to cover a few administrative matters before we get started. Firstly, please note that when I mention prices, I am referring to US dollars. Although I am Canadian, I think it's best to keep things simple and ensure we are comparing apples to apples! Also, as with all my books, I recommend you treat yourself to a pretty little journal to record your thoughts and ideas along our journey together. (The accountant in me never passes up an opportunity to make a case for good record keeping!) I'll be encouraging you to take notes regularly as we make our way through the chapters. If you are going to spend your precious time devising plans and doing research, you most certainly want to store the fruits of your labour in a safe and easily accessible place! Lastly, I should mention that I have no affiliations with any of the brands I mention in this book. I'm just a loyal fan!

The purpose of this book is to both inspire and inform you. I aim to trigger a sense of enthusiasm in you, while providing you with the tools and information you need to achieve second-hand success! It is meant to be a quick, zippy and energizing read, full of tricks and tips to kickstart and support your preloved fashion journey. The chapters are laid out with a bit of a flow in mind, but they are also designed to stand on their own. Depending on your current knowledge of and experience with preloved shopping, you may choose to jump around as it suits you. I must warn you, I am a list person! To that end, I have included a list of *Stylish Secrets* at the end of each chapter. I cap the whole book off by inviting you to tag along on one of my shopping trips!

Are you ready to jump on the second-hand fashion wagon with me? There's no time like the present, so grab that journal and let's get started!

1

PINPOINT YOUR PRIORITIES

There are many misconceptions about the preloved fashion market, so I thought I should start this book off with a sales pitch! I'm here to ignite both curiosity and enthusiasm in you, and sell you on the many benefits second-hand shopping has to offer.

I wasn't always a fan of preloved goods! As a child, I despised wearing my sister's hand-me-downs. Alas, as the youngest of two girls, her leftovers and castoffs were often relegated to my dresser drawers. I was great at dreaming up creative excuses as to why I simply couldn't wear them. Everything was either too itchy, too tight, too loose, too long, too short or too ugly (and in my mind, just too *used*). Back then, my talented and industrious mother actually sewed most of our clothing. (She was, after all, a home economics teacher.) I'm guessing she aimed to get as much mileage as possible out of her hard work. Mom always liked to sprinkle her creations with special finishing touches. Many of our handmade garments were persona-lized with our initials. (I know, so cute!) At least I could legitimately reject those items adorned with a "K" instead of a "J"!

As a teen, my attitude towards preloved clothing started to shift direction. My high school years fell smack in the middle of the grunge era. Style goals back then revolved around looking as disheveled and grungy (of course) as possible. An effortlessly cool and edgy aesthetic was achieved with plaid shirts, ripped jeans, work boots and oversized silhouettes. As you can imagine, highly distressed denim was a hot-ticket item. It wasn't that easy to come by, as this was before distressing was factory made. (Acid wash was definitely passé by this point in time!) If you were lusting after a pair of authentically worn-out jeans, you had to put in the hard work and wear and tear yourself!

My quest for a shortcut solution to my distressing dilemma turned me on to the second-hand mindset. At the time, my sister was attending university in the uber cool and stylish city of Montréal. She had access to some of the hippest thrift stores in the country! I sent her on a mission to find a pair of Levi's 501 jean shorts, and she did not disappoint. While home for Thanksgiving, she presented me with the most perfectly destroyed denim shorts I had ever laid eyes on. Someone had even embe-llished them with a few cool ink sketches (as well as a mysterious phone number…which I was convinced surely belonged to some super-hot French guy). This was my first taste of treasure hunting. My thrift store score opened my eyes to the fact that a trip to the mall wasn't always the answer to my fashion dilemmas.

There are so many compelling reasons why sourcing your clothing second-hand is a smart (and fun) way to shop. Getting a good handle on the perks of preloved fashion is a terrific way to inspire and motivate yourself to adopt a second-hand mindset.

Now is a good time to pull out your journal! As we walk through the benefits of second-hand shopping, make note of those arguments that really grab your attention. Pinpointing your personal motivations, and getting them down on paper, is an effective way to trigger a sense of enthusiasm inside you. Identifying your priorities early on in your journey will help keep you focused and inspired over the long term.

Save Money

Being an accountant, I can't help but kick off my sales pitch with a financial focus! You don't have to be a numbers girl like me to get excited about the notion of saving money. Money is a big motivator for the majority of us. No matter the size of your bank account, it makes sense to spend your money wisely. Stepping outside mainstream shopping avenues, and building your wardrobe with pre-loved garments, allows you to stretch your clothing budget.

We all want to get the most bang for our hard-earned bucks. The prices of garments available through second-hand avenues will vary depending on a number of factors, but as a general rule, they are usually set at one third of the original retail value. A handbag with a sticker price of $100 will likely carry a price tag of $30 at a consignment store. It doesn't take an accountant or mathematician to recognize that the opportunity for saving money is significant!

Even if you aren't running on a tight budget, as the old saying goes, "A penny saved is a penny earned." Funds that you might normally allocate towards your wardrobe can be redirected to savings, charity or other spending categories.

It's a fun exercise to go through a few hypothetical scenarios to drive home this point. Why not grab your journal and a calculator and walk yourself through a few calculations? How much money could you free up if you spent 50-70% less than your planned clothing allowance? Let's say your wardrobe budget is $1,000. If you were able to tick everything off your shopping list for even half of that, what would you do with the $500 savings? Maybe you could afford that new winter coat you figured would have to wait until next year. You might choose to tuck the leftover money into a vacation fund, or make a satisfying lump-sum payment on your mortgage. I'm guessing you won't have trouble finding a use for some extra cash!

Being a good steward of your money means making financial decisions with care and intention. Choosing to shop the preloved marketplace can certainly help you advance on your financial goals.

Consume Sustainably

I'm not going to pretend that I am an eco-warrior who lives a perfectly environmentally friendly lifestyle. That being said, I am deeply concerned about the state of our planet, and try to act in ways that minimize my personal ecological footprint.

We are all familiar with the motto, "Reduce, Reuse, Recycle". When it comes to curating an environmentally friendly wardrobe, the *best* thing you can do is *reduce* your consumption (brand new or preloved). Over the last forty years, the rise of fast fashion has normalized ridiculously discounted price tags and overstuffed closets. We've been conditioned to believe that our clothes need to be fresh, trendy, cheap and abundant.

While reducing our overall consumption of clothing should be our main earth-friendly focus, *reusing* garments and accessories is the next best option! The preloved fashion market recirculates items, and therefore extends their lives. This in turn helps lighten the load on landfills and shifts demand away from producers of new garments. When you purchase a piece of used clothing, you are granting it a second chance at life! It's a win-win situation for everyone (except the fast fashion retailers).

The political, ethical and environmental issues surrounding the fashion industry are complex and extend beyond the scope of this book. If this is a topic you are interested in or passionate about, I suggest you dig deeper. The documentary, *True Cost* is a great starting point. It certainly improved my awareness of the issues surrounding the fashion industry, and inspired me to fill my closet with more sustainable choices. Educating yourself on the environmental and social impacts of mainstream fashion can serve as motivation to adopt a second-hand shopping strategy. Tapping into the preloved market is a small, tangible contribution that you can make as an individual consumer. There is something gratifying about acting in ways that lessen the negative impact on our planet.

Elevate Your Style

The preloved market provides access to garments that might normally be outside your budget. Second-hand shopping is my most powerful secret weapon for elevating my style! It allows me to welcome high-end and high-quality items into my wardrobe for a fraction of the full retail cost.

Wearing well-constructed garments and footwear made with quality materials gives your outfits a more polished, pulled-together and elevated look. High-quality items also tend to last much longer, so you will be able to enjoy them for years to come. Buying pieces that can withstand the test of time offers a triple crown win! You elevate your style, improve your bank balance, and lessen your impact on Mother Earth...win-win-win.

I have a bit of an obsession for Italian footwear, with one of my favorite brands being Fiorentini+Baker. Their artisan-made styles are comfortable, high quality, edgy and yet classic. They are also quite pricey, with most boots ranging from $400 to $500. I'm not arguing with the price! You definitely get what you pay for...unless of course you snag a pair on the used market for $55 as I did last fall. My new-to-me boots are stunning and add an elevated finishing touch to my outfits. They will be valuable members of my wardrobe for many, many years to come. I don't think I could say the same if I'd spent the $55 on a pair from the discount store at the mall!

Set Yourself Apart

Shopping outside the mainstream avenues allows you to build a wardrobe that is unique and original. Because most used goods hail from past seasons, you won't look like you just went on a shopping spree at the mall. Creating a wardrobe that includes a few special, rare and unusual pieces will prevent you from looking like a carbon copy of everyone else walking the streets. Let's face it, standing out a bit can feel delicious!

Just because something is old doesn't mean it is dated or out of style. High-quality, classic pieces transcend trends and fads. One of my favorite garments that I receive the most compliments on is an army-green wool surplus jacket by the Canadian designer Smythe. It's from their 2009 collection (which makes it thirteen years old at the time this book is being written). This jacket is a gem that will never go out of style. It includes a lot of distinctive details that really set it apart. The fabric is a thick, rich wool. The zipper and buttons are heavy duty, and a set of metal D-rings cinch the waist at just the right spot to provide a flattering silhouette. Smythe jackets normally retail for $700 to $800, but I picked up this beauty for an incredible deal at $80.

Enjoy the Hunt

I remember reading somewhere that one of the most enjoyable aspects of a vacation is actually the anticipation of it! There is something to be said about savoring the sweetness of looking forward to something.

In our world of instant gratification, it feels like we are growing more impatient by the day! Shifting your perspective, and exercising more patience, allows you to shop with more purpose, care and intention. Second-hand shopping forces you to slow down. It's about finding both joy and reward in the *process,* instead of just the result. The hunt becomes as valuable as the prize.

Sourcing items on the preloved market is modern-day treasure hunting! Doesn't that sound like a lot of fun? There are some pieces I've waited for *years* to pop up on the second-hand marketplace. There is a sweet sense of satisfaction when you finally get your hands on a highly-coveted and long-awaited item. By resisting the urge to settle, and bypassing less-ideal options while you wait, you will be rewarded for your patience with something you value and cherish. You will be more likely to appreciate it and take good care of it over the long run (and again experience positive financial and environmental impacts!)

STYLISH SECRETS

- Look for ways to inspire yourself into following through on your journey into the second-hand market. Identify your *why* and write it down as a reminder to yourself.

- What benefits of second-hand shopping are you most passionate about? Take the time to learn the advantages of choosing preloved over new. Identify how they tie into your values and goals.

- Shopping second-hand is a money-saving strategy! How might you rework your clothing budget if you were able to acquire items on your wish list at a discounted price? As an accountant, I recommend doing the calculations. The numbers can be inspiring!

- Choosing second-hand over new represents a tangible way you can consume more sustainably. Use this knowledge as fuel to inspire yourself to alter your shopping habits.

- Tapping into the preloved market is a fabulous way to elevate your style. You will be able to add high-quality pieces to your wardrobe that might normally be outside your budget.

- Enjoy the creative aspects of shopping second-hand. Sourcing unique and original items will set you apart and help you stand out in a crowd.

- Recognize that shopping second-hand requires patience. Treasure hunting is fun!

2

OPEN YOUR MIND

Hopefully my sales pitch in the last chapter won you over. You are 100% convinced and ready to jump in so you can start reaping the benefits of second-hand shopping! If you are more of a skeptic like me, you might find yourself hanging on to feelings of apprehension, confusion and doubt. Perhaps you fully recognize and believe the advantages of delving into the preloved market, but you still feel nervous and hesitant. Although the concepts and arguments make sense, you aren't convinced that shopping second-hand is right for *you*.

If you are feeling a bit tentative to step outside the comfort zone of mainstream shopping methods, please hear me out. I'm about to turn up the heat on my sales pitch. There are a myriad of reasons why people instinctively turn their noses up at the notion of welcoming preloved clothing into their wardrobes. I'm going to walk you through some of the most common myths many of us encounter.

(I'm including myself here!) I'm hoping my arguments might soon have any apprehensive readers singing a different tune!

Myth #1: I'm interested, but I don't know where to start!

If you've never experimented with shopping second-hand, it can seem a little scary at first. Again, I felt the exact same way when I was first starting out. I was excited about the concept of welcoming preloved goods into my wardrobe, but I didn't know where to start. Like a deer in the headlights, I felt frozen and unsure of which direction to move first.

You've taken the first step of your journey by picking up this book. I'm going to gently walk you through some fun and easy starter strategies for rookies in chapter 8. Your first success will no doubt leave you craving for more!

Myth #2: I'm not cool, creative or artsy.

I used to think only cool, hip or extremely lucky people could find success in second-hand shops. Certain people have a knack for identifying the creative potential of a garment and how it would fit fabulously into their eclectic collection of clothing. These are the people who could probably create a stylish ensemble out of a bed sheet and a ball cap. I'll be very clear. I am *not* one of these people, and I never will be! As I mentioned, I'm an everyday woman. Like many women, I struggled for years to compile a wardrobe that made me feel good on the inside *and* the outside!

Ten years ago, I found myself facing a style and identity crisis. As a stay-at-home mom in my mid-thirties, I was completely immersed in my demanding role of raising two busy toddlers. I was putting almost zero effort into my personal appearance, and my self-esteem was at an all-time low. For years I sloshed around in ill-fitting jeans, hoodies and yoga pants. My personal style goals were non-existent!

Recognizing I needed to take action, I set off on a journey to elevate my personal style and improve my sense of self-worth. My book, *Elevate Your Personal Style: Inspiration for the Everyday Woman,* details the steps I undertook to transform both my outward appearance and my inner landscape. (I recommend you check it out!) As I started to sink my teeth into the task of building a wardrobe I truly loved, I quickly realized there was a huge gap between my style goals and my budget! I believe humans have an intrinsic attraction to beautiful things. When I walk into a store, I seem to be magnetically drawn to high-quality, gorgeous items that, unsurprisingly, usually carry a hefty price tag. I knew I was in for a challenge, and started to seek out creative ways to fulfill my wish list, while staying within budget.

Shopping on the second-hand market was an obvious strategy. I was no stranger to sourcing used goods, and was well aware of the cost-saving benefits. We had just built a home that incorporated a fair amount of reclaimed building materials. Nostalgic by nature, we decided to furnish it mainly with antiques. I was also frequenting the local second-hand shops to source affordable fashion for my quickly growing boys. Despite this, I had higher style standards for myself than the kids. I was skeptical that preloved shopping for my own wardrobe was going to measure up!

I also didn't feel confident in my *ability* to source suitable garments for myself. As an everyday woman, the idea of building a wardrobe with preloved pieces felt unattainable and inaccessible. I was doubtful it was an area I could succeed!

If you share the same sentiment I did, please stick with me! I'm going to show you exactly how I convinced myself to open my mind to preloved options, and how I learned that this method of shopping is accessible to *everyone*. There is no right or wrong way to approach it. You are the one in charge, so you get to make the rules. You have the freedom to create a customized shopping strategy based on your personality, skills, goals and budget. My plan is to give you all the information you need to do so!

I realize now that I underestimated myself and my abilities, because I had labelled myself as plain and boring in the style department. In fact, I believe organized and analytical personality types are just as suited for second-hand shopping as those who are more creatively inclined. Everyone has strengths to bring to the table.

Myth #3: Used clothing is dirty and gross.

During my late twenties, I spent most of my weekends rummaging through the mountainous bins of used clothing stores. I wasn't treasure hunting for my wardrobe, but was instead in search of craft supplies! In an effort to add some homespun charm to our new house, I had taken up rug hooking as a hobby. This traditional craft originated as a chore of necessity. Back in the day, women transformed old fabric scraps into rugs as a way to add warmth to their cold, barren floors. Wanting to stay true to the original craft, I sourced most of my rug hooking supplies at the second-hand shops, keeping an eye out for the perfect color and texture of fabric that I could piece together into a little work of art. (Maybe I was a little artsy after all and didn't even recognize it!)

When I first set sail on my personal style journey, the recollection of those dingy bins from my rug hooking days left a bad taste in my mouth (or nose). I couldn't shake the nauseating smell of those shops from my memory! I would describe it as a cocktail of fabric softener, moth balls, dust and body odor. This was *not* a signature scent that was going to elevate my style!

For many people, the concept of wearing someone else's clothes might feel kind of creepy, gross or unsanitary. I felt the same way, until I investigated the situation a little further. What I learned, is that the second-hand market includes many brand new, unworn and minimally used items. You just have to know how and where to find them! *These* are the treasures I personally seek out, and the tips and tricks I offer in this book are going to help you do the same. I assure you, I'm not in the market for anything that should be relegated to the rag bin, and I'm not suggesting you should be either.

Myth #4: Second-hand shopping is overwhelming and difficult.

If you have visions of overflowing bins of used clothing as I did, the possibility of finding a diamond in the rough feels overwhelming, if not impossible. Again, I carried the same mental image, until the day I stepped into one of my local consignment shops. At first glance, one would never have known it was a second-hand shop. This chic little boutique was tastefully decorated and beautifully organized with inspiring displays. There was nothing overwhelming about the shop's layout or environment. The racks were sorted by size, color and type of garment, so it was easy for me to zone in on my area of interest.

The clothes were clean and in excellent condition, many with the original tags still attached!

No, this was not the sort of place you might magically unearth a Gucci jacket for $14.99. The price tags were still relatively high, but I knew enough to recognize they were heavily discounted. Consignment shops definitely offer an elevated shopping experience that makes the preloved market more approachable and accessible to everyday women like us!

Shopping online for preloved goods is another fabulous option that isn't as complicated as you might think. I'll get into more detail on this topic in chapter 5, but for now I want to point out that shopping second-hand online can be slick, easy, efficient and successful! It's my main method of shopping, so stay tuned. I have lots of stylish secrets to share on the topic.

Myth #5: I don't have the time to shop second-hand.

Our society's obsession with instant gratification means we have access to whatever we want, whenever we want it! Yes, choosing to go the second-hand route may require you to exercise your patience muscles. The exact item you are in search of might not be immediately available.

That being said, shopping second-hand doesn't have to suck up every last minute of your spare time. There is no need to spend all your weekends scouring the used cloth-ing stores and consignment shops (unless this is something you genuinely enjoy). There are a number of secrets to shopping smart and efficiently that I'm excited to share with you!

STYLISH SECRETS

- It is important to maintain an open mind and clear out the mental roadblocks we set up for ourselves around preloved goods.

- There is no need to feel intimidated by second-hand shopping. If you are new to the game, starting out gently is the way to go. The tips you learn in this book will tee you up for success! Recognize that creating a wardrobe with second-hand finds is a fun and rewarding experience that is accessible to all of us.

- Second-hand shopping is not reserved for a certain type of person. We all have strengths that we can use to make our shopping efforts successful.

- Second-hand, preloved and preowned are misleading terms. Many items available on the aftermarket sat in someone's closet lonely and unworn. It's not hard to find garments that are practically (or actually!) brand new with no signs of wear.

- Shopping second-hand isn't overwhelming if you know the right places to look. Consignment shops (brick-and-mortar and/or virtual) are usually set up to offer the same experience as a mainstream boutique.

- Sourcing your preloved goods might require more patience, but it doesn't necessarily require a large investment of your time. There are a number of strategies to help streamline the process and make your search run more efficiently and smoothly.

3

EXPLORE THE LANDSCAPE

It's rarely a good idea to set off on a new journey without peering to the horizon and assessing the landscape ahead of you. The terrain of the preloved market differs from the conventional shopping avenues most of us are well acquainted with.

If you are used to shopping at the mall, or buying clothes online from traditional retailers, you might be feeling a bit intimidated. I'm here to help! I'm going to point you in the right direction and get you headed down the path of your second-hand shopping journey.

A research project is a fun, informative and inspiring way to kick off your preloved fashion adventure. (It's definitely a wise step to take before pulling out your credit card for the first flashy thing you cross paths with.) Take some time to familiarize yourself with the preloved apparel market and the opportunities it has to offer. What is available in your local community? What are the different online shopping options and how do they compare? How do the prices for used goods compare to regular retail pricing? This upfront research will provide you with a greater level of comfort when it comes time to make a purchase, and will also help you make informed and wise decisions when choosing to add a piece to your wardrobe.

Explore Brick-and-Mortar Options

There is a quiet revolution taking place in the land of clothing resale. Consumers are increasingly opening their minds, closets and wallets to the opportunities offered by the preloved fashion market. As a result, more and more used clothing stores are popping up in the landscape. These days, most cities, towns and communities have at least one thrift or consignment store within striking distance.

Although we live in a digital age, there are still many advantages to shopping in person. First, spending your money within your community helps support local business owners. Second, nothing beats examining an item with your five senses (or at least three of them). Not only does shopping at a brick-and-mortar store allow you to try pieces on, but it gives you the opportunity to thoroughly examine your selections for damage, wear and odour!

Second-hand clothing stores come in all shapes, styles and sizes! They range from overflowing thrift and charity shops, to carefully curated, high-end consignment bou-tiques. Get to know the stores in your community. Visiting your local shops in person will give you a good idea of what type of inventory they carry and how it is organized and displayed. Your sleuthing should help you answer a few key questions. Do they carry the styles and brands you are interested in? Is there a nice selection of items available in your size? Are the prices reasonable and within your budget? Is the inventory easy to sort through? Are the garments clean and in good condition? With this valuable information in hand, you can determine which shops best suit your style, personality, budget and lifestyle.

Thrift Shops

As I mentioned previously, I was no stranger to thrift shops when I began my own personal style journey. I spent years combing them for both craft supplies and children's clothing. Every now and then I'd wander over to the women's department and casually flick through the racks.

I aim to be as authentic as possible, so I'm going to be very honest about my experience with these types of shops. I've never had much luck finding clothing for myself in thrift stores. That pair of Levi's cut-offs I mentioned in chapter 2 was one of just two fashion thrift store scores (and technically, my sister did the treasure hunting, so she should be credited with the win).

If you read my book *Elevate Your Life at Home,* you might be able to guess my other big thrifted score. It's an invaluable and hard-working garment I've had in my closet for over seventeen years, and will likely never part with! I managed to snag a cute little mechanic's suit from our old provincial phone company that, unbelievably, fits my 5'3" frame perfectly! I wear it every time I find myself faced with a heavy-duty household task (painting, piling wood, gardening). It's even served as a Halloween costume on more than one occasion. If it weren't covered in paint, I could probably pull off wearing it in public. It definitely ticks the box on the jumpsuit/boilersuit fashion trend!

Even though my personal thrifting successes are limited, this doesn't mean you should cross this option off *your* list! I don't want to deter you from exploring this valuable source for preowned fashion. There are several advantages to thrift stores, and they offer an amazing opportunity for many people.

When it comes to used clothing, thrift shop pricing tends to be the most competitive. Their lower prices will allow you to stretch your fashion budget to the maximum! If you have a good eye for spotting a diamond in the rough, thrift shops will suit you perfectly. This seems to be where I fell short. I had great difficulty finding gems amongst the confusing clutter. That being said, some thrift stores I've visited were actually pretty neat and organized. I've seen shops on all levels of the organizational spectrum, so it's important to check out your local spots and assess the situation in person.

Going the thrift shop route can definitely involve a time commitment. Whether this is a deterrent for you really depends on your approach and perspective. Some people genuinely enjoy cruising crammed racks and bins in search of hidden nuggets. I can definitely relate to the thrill of the hunt. I've always been an admirer of antique furniture. There's nothing I love more than spending a leisurely afternoon sifting through dusty, musty antique shops in search of a unique item to decorate my home. If this form of treasure hunting classifies as one of your hobbies, then the idea of spending an afternoon scouring thrift shops might sound dreamy!

Consignment Stores

I'm a huge fan of consignment stores! I've experienced great success with them, both as a consignor and a customer. As I mentioned in chapter 2, my first visit to one of my local consignment boutiques was a huge eye opener for me, and served as a turning point in my personal style journey.

In my opinion, consignment boutiques offer the best of both worlds. They provide access to amazing preloved fashion, while still delivering the pleasant and inspiring shopping experience we tend to associate with traditional retail stores.

The consignment shops I've visited have been well organized, clean, tastefully decorated and beautifully appointed with pretty dressing rooms, great lighting and lots of mirrors. As small businesses, they offer a more unique, charming and inspiring environment than the chain stores at the mall!

Most consignment boutiques set high standards for what products they allow through their doors. Stores vary on the brands they accept, but most consignment shops only take on goods that are in excellent condition with minimal signs of wear. If you aren't into the yard-sale vibe of thrift stores, then I suspect consignment boutiques will suit your style!

On the downside, prices at consignment stores definitely tend to run higher than at their thrift shop counterparts. If you are in search of bargain basement pricing, you won't likely find it among the racks of a consignment boutique. Pricing strategies vary depending on the brand and condition of an item. As a general rule, you can usually pick something up for a third of the original retail price, which still represents huge savings!

The availability of brands and styles will depend largely on where you live. In most instances, your neighbourhood store is stocked directly from the closets of the surrounding community. Consignment shops offer a very convenient and hassle-free way to monetize closet castoffs! (I'll expand more on this in chapter 10.) I live in the small Canadian city of Halifax, Nova Scotia, which has a population of just over 450,000. Although it's a far cry from the fashion capital of the world, my local shops still carry a decent selection of brands and sizes.

Most shops maintain social media pages. Scrolling through their Instagram feeds will provide you with a taste of their offerings. From there you can determine whether an in-person visit is worth your time and effort.

Explore the Online Shopping Scene

Consumer shopping habits are definitely undergoing a rapid transformation, accelerated even more by the global pandemic. The popularity of online shopping is growing at record speed. I can think of very few things you can't acquire online! The fact that one can shop virtually for heirloom tomatoes says it all. I just finished filling my virtual shopping cart with an order of fresh garden veggies. With just the click of a button, they will be delivered to my doorstep by a small farm down the road.

An increased interest in sustainability, paired with society's online shopping obsession, has resulted in a burgeoning virtual marketplace for preloved apparel. The selection and sheer quantity of options is actually rather overwhelming!

Does online shopping best suit your lifestyle? Perhaps you run a busy schedule, and doing your shopping virtually allows you to manage your time more effectively.

Maybe you simply enjoy the convenience and ease of shopping from the comfort of your home. If you live in or near a big metropolitan centre, chances are you can get your hands on pretty much anything and everything your heart desires. Such is not the case for those of us who live less urban lifestyles. In-person shopping options (and in particular, high-end consignment fashion), are often limited in small towns or rural settings. Even though my local community boasts a handful of lovely consignment boutiques, they don't always carry the selection of brands and sizes I'm looking for.

As a Francophile, I tend to gravitate towards a number of European brands that are not readily available on this side of the pond. This might just be a case of "the grass is always greener" syndrome. Perhaps those of you living in Europe are trying to get your hands on North American brands! Regardless, I am infatuated with a number of French brands that are very difficult to source in my local area. Because the retail shops where I live don't carry them, they rarely pop up in the consignment stores. Some of these brands include Des Petits Hauts, Sézane, Repetto, A.P.C, Rouje, ba&sh, Vanessa Bruno, Isabel Marant, Maje... etc. (I could go on and on, but you get the idea!) Shopping for preloved fashion online definitely opens the door of opportunity, no matter where you live.

The plethora of options, however, can be a bit intimidating if you are new to the preloved shopping game.

Extending your research project to the digital market-place is an important step to familiarize yourself with the options available, and the pros and cons of each. This will allow you to narrow in on online sources that best suit your needs.

Before I get started on discussing the online pre-owned fashion market, I need to point out that I am a Canadian. I can only speak from my own personal experience, which is obviously going to have a North American flavour. I'm here to provide you with a starting point for your research. The list I'm going to walk through is not all inclusive by any stretch. Fashion resale is an evolving market with new shops and sites popping up all the time!

As you go through my list and start researching the various options, here are a few key questions to consider and make note of:

- Does this shopping platform offer shipping to your geographical area? (Canada is often excluded from American and European options.)
- Where are the goods shipping from? Will there be additional and unexpected charges for shipping, duties and taxes if they are being sent from a foreign country?
- Are you able to ask the seller questions? There are times you might want additional photos or measurements, so it's always nice when you can communicate directly with the seller.

- What are the return policies?
- Are there any controls in place to ensure that the item is authentic and as advertised?

eBay

Most of us are familiar with eBay, as it has likely been around the longest. It's where I made some of my first preloved fashion purchases. I was in the market for a pair of Frye boots, and the selection on eBay at the time was excellent. The eBay platform is pretty easy to navigate if you know specifically what you are looking for. I'm always sure to read the seller reviews carefully before making a purchase. It's easy and simple to contact the seller directly if you need additional information on an item. Return policies vary by seller.

Etsy

A lot of us associate Etsy with handmade goods. In fact, my first experience on Etsy was as a seller. I ran a little shop called *The Wool Fairy* for a few years. When my children were young, I used to knit and crochet natural toys out of wool, which I sold both online and at local craft fairs. Years down the road, I realized that Etsy is a fabulous source for vintage fashion items. Their selection of estate jewelry is amazing. I have a small collection of solid-gold hoop earrings I purchased on this site. I also picked up a classic vintage Longchamp crossbody bag that was in mint condition.

Direct from Seller Sites

There are tons of sites that facilitate sales transactions directly between the buyer and seller. Although purchases are made through the platform, there is no middleman (or middlewoman) handling the items. The seller posts the items for sale, sets the prices, and ships directly to the buyer. Communicating and negotiating with the seller is easy. The rules around returns and guaranteeing authenticity depend on the site.

Poshmark, Tradesy, Depop, Vestiaire Collective and Vinted all fall under this category. Each one of these resale platforms is unique, so you will need to spend some time reading the fine print and getting comfortable with their policies and procedures.

For instance, sales on Vinted are shipped directly from seller to buyer. Vestiaire Collective, on the other hand, adds an extra layer of buyer protection in their process. All sales flow through an inspection center before being approved and shipped to the customer.

I once purchased a silk blouse through Vestiaire Collective that looked picture perfect online. When it arrived at the inspection centre, however, it was rejected for having large sweat stains under the arm pits! I was notified of this breach in quality standards and was immediately issued a refund. This suited me just fine. No one wants to smell like BO, especially someone else's! I was thankful for this additional layer of protection they offered.

The availability of these sites depends on where you live. For instance, Tradesy does not ship to Canada, so that one is out for me. Poshmark is available in Canada, but I'm restricted to purchasing solely from Canadian sellers. Vestiaire Collective, which was founded in Paris, does allow shipping to North America! This is great news for any fellow Francophiles. What better way to dress like a French girl than to dive directly into her closet and scoop up her hand-me-downs?

Consignment Sites

There is another class of online platform that operates with a bit of involvement from a middleman. They are essentially the virtual equivalent of a classic consignment shop. The RealReal, and thredUP fall under this category.

In some instances, sellers (consignors) ship their items to the consignee, who then examines them for quality and authenticity. The consignee site takes the photos, posts the descriptions and ships to the buyer. Once an item sells, the consignor receives her share of the cut!

Snuggle up with a cup of tea and your phone and spend some time exploring the online options that offer shipping to your region. All these sites have apps that are very easy to navigate. Experiment with a few searches for a couple of items you might be interested in and see what pops up! Again, since I'm usually on the lookout for European brands, I often find what I'm looking for on Vestiaire Collective. Have fun investigating what sites best suit your style, needs and budget.

Small Business Sites

Of course, we must not forget all the hard-working small business owners out there! Many small consignment shops maintain websites with ecommerce capabilities. A lot of them also use social media platforms to advertise their inventory. I've direct-messaged small boutiques on occasion and have arranged payment and shipping for an item through PayPal. There are too many to list here! If you aren't sure where to start, try searching a few of these hashtags on Instagram and see where it leads you: #consignment #consignmentshop, #consignmentboutique. I tend to focus on Canadian boutiques, as this limits the dreaded duties and taxes!

Traditional Retailers

Consumers aren't the only ones exhibiting a growing interest in the fashion resale market. Traditional brands are starting to jump on the bandwagon as well, with many of them offering preowned options. I wasn't at all surprised to see an eco-conscious brand like Patagonia doing this. In fact, they have been promoting their "Worn Wear" program since as far back as 2013! What's amazing is that so many retailers are following their lead. Nike offers preloved kicks through its program "Refurbished". You can treat yourself to a classic pair of new-to-you Levi's at www.second-hand.levi.com. I was fascinated to discover that the large Canadian department store, The Bay, is peddling preloved designer handbags! (The Bay is basically Canada's version of Nordstrom.) Consumer demand for more sustainable options is definitely causing companies to adjust their business models!

Less Conventional Sources

There are so many creative and innovative ways for individuals to connect over preloved fashion. Clothing swaps are a fun way to refresh your wardrobe without spending a cent! Many people are selling preloved pieces directly from their own social media accounts, as well as online classified forums. The options and opportunities are endless once you start digging.

STYLISH SECRETS

- Get acquainted with the preloved fashion market. Challenge yourself to embark on a little research project! Explore your local second-hand shops as well as the various online shopping options.

- When visiting brick-and-mortar stores, flick through the racks and make note of the sizes, brands, styles and quality of the goods offered for sale. Is the store organized in a fashion that suits your shopping style?

- Thrift shops are a great option if you have both time and a good eye for spotting treasures. Prices in thrift shops tend to be the most competitive.

- Consignment boutiques are usually easier to navigate. They tend to offer higher quality items, but at steeper prices.

- The online shopping options for preloved fashion are growing by the day! They open the door of opportunity to access fabulous second-hand finds, no matter where you live.

- The list of options provided in this book can serve as a starting point for you. As you peruse the different sites, make note of information that feels important and relevant to you. Is the platform user friendly and easy to navigate? What brands are offered? Where are the items shipping from? Are you able to ask the seller questions? What is the return policy?

4

POWER UP WITH INFORMATION

I've always been drawn to the age-old saying by Sir Francis Bacon, "Knowledge itself is power." I love the idea of powering myself up with an arsenal of facts! It's probably one of the reasons I gravitated towards the accounting profession. Accounting is basically the compiling of financial information in a format that allows for informed decision making. No matter what decision you might be facing in life, doing your research and gathering reliable and relevant facts will provide you with valuable insights.

You can plug into the information power source when buying a new car, negotiating a mortgage, selecting a healthcare provider and yes, even much less consequential decisions, such as those concerning your wardrobe! Choosing whether or not to snatch up that fabulous (and heavily discounted) pair of preloved designer boots on thredUP might seem like an insignificant decision on its' own. From a big picture perspective, however, all your small purchasing decisions add up over time and have a substantial impact on your financial health.

When it comes to shopping for preloved fashion specifically, investing some time upfront to gather key information is a wise move. This initial strategic effort will save you both time and money in the long run. A thorough understanding of your own style goals, brand preferences, measurements and body type will serve you well. This knowledge will be instrumental in helping you make successful purchases that fit your body, personal style and quality standards. Informed decisions are *usually* good decisions! A solid set of personal fashion facts (stored safely in your trusty style journal) also helps to streamline the preloved shopping process. You will be able to hone your hunting techniques to zero in on your wish list more efficiently.

Know Thyself

How well acquainted are you with your body? Keeping track of your physical measurements is a critical success factor, particularly when shopping for preloved goods online. When the opportunity to try on a garment is not available, reaching for the measuring tape is the next best option. Online sellers usually provide measurements of the garments they have listed for sale. You can also refer to brand-specific size charts to compare your measurements to the piece you have your eye on.

That tape measure kicking around the toolbox isn't going to cut it. You will need the proper tool in order to take accurate measurements. If you don't have one already, invest in an inexpensive sewing tape made of flexible fabric or plastic. They are available at both craft and dollar stores.

I have a record of my *bust, shoulders, waist, low waist, hips and inseam* measurements in both centimeters and inches. Since I've purchased the odd hat online, I also have my *head circumference* recorded in my notebook. Knowing your *ring size(s)* is also useful information if you are a jewelry enthusiast. I picked up a cheap ring sizer off Amazon. I had a signet ring custom made and I needed to provide my size to the designer. It's a nice item to have on hand, but you can also go into any jewelry store and have your fingers measured.

If you aren't quite sure how to take proper measurements, a quick search on YouTube will have you enlightened. It's also important to note that our measurements can change over time as we gain or lose weight, or simply move into another season of life. Updating your measurements once or twice a year will ensure you are working with accurate numbers!

Collect Brand Specific Research

The vast majority of my preloved purchases are from brands I'm already familiar with. Being well acquainted with those specific brands that suit your personal style, budget and quality standards helps ensure success when shopping the preloved market. Your past experiences with, and knowledge of the brand, will allow you to make informed decisions about styles, sizes, fit and prices.

I like to develop a fairly intimate relationship with my favorite brands. The more detailed information you can gather on a particular item, the greater the chance of tracking it down on the preloved market and being pleased with your purchase.

For instance, I have a number of pieces from the brand Equipment in my wardrobe. Their silk blouses and cashmere sweaters are chic, high quality and timeless. I've been 100% satisfied with every thrifted purchase from this brand. (In fact, every single piece of Equipment clothing in my wardrobe was acquired on the preloved market.) I owe some of my success to the time and effort I invested in research.

As you get to know a few brands and explore their prices on the preloved market, you can start to compile a list of labels that suit your style *and* budget. The preloved market offers opportunities at every price point, from H&M to Chanel!

Seek Out Inspiration

At this point, your mind may have just slammed into a concrete wall. Maybe you have absolutely no clue what brands are out there, and which ones would suit your personal style. I can relate! This was definitely my situation early on in my own style journey. I didn't have any *favorite brands*, as my meagre wardrobe consisted mainly of faded, misshapen t-shirts and ill-fitting jeans. I had just popped out two babies seventeen months apart. My corporate attire from my office job consisted of maternity wear.

In a desperate effort to clothe my body in *something*, I distinctly remember pushing the double baby stroller into Old Navy and grabbing the same long-sleeve t-shirt in six colors, along with two pairs of jeans I estimated would fit. Too exhausted and frazzled to attempt a visit to the dressing room with my gargantuan stroller and screaming children, I was through the checkout and out the door in record time. This shopping strategy was on repeat, as after a few months of wear, the shrunken, faded and stained shirts needed replacing. The only thing I knew for certain was that I didn't need or want any more t-shirts from Old Navy!

I was determined to up my style game, but again, I had no idea where to start. This is when I discovered the wonderful world of Pinterest! It's a fantastic platform to explore personal style and visually define your likes and dislikes. If you are struggling with where to begin as I was, I recommend you spend some time seeking out inspiration and getting in touch with the clothing aesthetic that captures your heart.

I actually started with doing searches on some of my favorite celebrities. Jennifer Aniston was one of my first fashion muses. I admired her California cool vibe and her streetstyle looks. As a Francophile, a search on "French girl style" popped up results featuring style icons such as Emmanuelle Alt and Clemence Poésy.

Once you have a collection of inspiring images pinned to a board, you can start to zero in on the brand details. Certainly, celebrities are often spotted wearing luxury designer labels that carry exorbitant prices (new or used!). Although celebrity style might seem out of reach at first glance, it can be surprisingly accessible on the second-hand market. With a bit of sleuthing on Google and Pinterest, you can often uncover the precise details of garments worn by the Hollywood crowd. For instance, if you are into royal fashion, you have no further to look than sites like www.whatkatewore.com or www.whatmeghanwore.net. Kate Middleton and Meghan Markle are actually known for wearing accessible brands such as Everlane and J. Crew.

I fell in love with a pair of boots I eyed on Jennifer Aniston. A search through www.celebritystyleguide.com helped me identify the brand as Fiorentini+Baker (which

I had never heard of at the time). Jennifer's "Eternity" boots retail for around $500, but I was able to pick up mine for $100 on eBay.

Fashion bloggers and YouTubers also offer ample inspiration and information when it comes to discovering new brands. After reading *Lessons from Madame Chic* by Jennifer L. Scott, I tuned into her YouTube channel. This is where I was first introduced to the brands Equipment and APC. They are both high-quality brands with expensive price tags, but I've managed to fill my wardrobe with a number of amazing pieces by taking the budget-friendly, second-hand route.

Lastly, seek information and inspiration from those chic and stylish people around you! I have one particular neighbour/friend who oozes style and grace. I wasn't shy to piggyback on her talent and knowledge early on in my research. I often quizzed her about her favorite shops and brands. If you spot a woman in a fabulous coat at the grocery checkout, why not pay her a compliment and ask her where she purchased it? Most people will feel flattered by the attention and will be more than happy to divulge their style secrets.

Investigate Your Own Closet

An excellent source of brand information is often your very own closet. I use my style journal to maintain an inventory list of all the items in my wardrobe. One of the reasons I do this is to keep track of those brands that are currently working well for me. Can you identify certain brands that you already wear and love? If so, you already know what sizes and styles suit your body. Finding duplicates or similar items on the second-hand market is a lot easier if you are already comfortable with a specific garment.

When it came time to add a pair of navy blue ballet flats to my wardrobe, I immediately knew the brand, size and style that would fit my needs perfectly. I already owned an ideal pair in black, so it was just a matter of hitting the repeat button. I did a quick search for my favorite Repetto "Cendrillon" ballet flats in size 38.5 and located a preloved pair (in mint condition) on Vestiaire Collective in no time.

I keep a log in my style journal of those items in my closet that I adore, so that when it comes time to replace or duplicate, I know *exactly* what I'm looking for.

Browse the Shops In Person

Other times, you might be interested in testing out a new brand that has caught your attention. Getting up close and personal with new brands by examining them in person is the ideal scenario, if you can swing it.

A few years ago, I went on a quick getaway to Toronto with my husband. He was travelling for work, so I decided to tag along for a couple of days. I've lived in Canada my entire life, and this was my very first trip to the big city! We spent most of our time sightseeing, but I also viewed it as an opportunity to partake in a little shopping. I was in the market for a pair of Swedish Hasbeens clogs, which were not available in my hometown city of Halifax. They were a pricy item that I wanted to try on and examine in person before making any big decisions.

I ended up with a few hours on my own to kill downtown, and found myself walking through the doors of our country's big department store, The Bay. While I had already exhausted my budget for the trip, I jumped at the opportunity to gather some research.

I spent about two hours trying on clothing just for the fun. I focused my attention on the Equipment section of the floor as I was curious about this brand after learning about it from Jennifer L. Scott. I had never seen its offerings in person, so this was my chance! Thankfully, I had my trusty style journal in my handbag and was able to record my findings. I noted the retail prices, names and colorways of the specific garments that caught my eye. Taking the time to try things on, even though I didn't intend to purchase them in that moment, gave me valuable information. Now I knew with certainty that I was size extra small in their "Slim Signature Silk Shirt". I determined that I preferred a roomier fit in their cashmere sweaters, so would want to size up to a small in the "Sloan" and "Oscar" styles. I also took the time to snap a few quick photos in the dressing room, that I could later upload to my Pinterest boards.

When the time came to indulge in a new cashmere sweater, I had no problem finding a size small Equipment "Sloane" crewneck on eBay in the color "peacoat". Since I knew it carried a retail price tag of $300, I was able to determine that the $75 I paid for it was more than reasonable.

Some people may have mixed feelings about this approach to brand research. To my surprise, I discovered there is actually a name for it! Apparently, it's referred to as "showrooming" in retail circles, and is described as the consumer practice of examining goods in person in a brick-and-mortar shop, only to return home and buy them online (usually at a lower price). It's important for me to note that I would never adopt this approach at a small business. I really value the outstanding customer service offered by my favorite local boutiques. My own wardrobe is a mix of both new and preloved pieces. Most of my new items were purchased at small local shops, and I genuinely enjoy supporting them with my business! Because it was very much a self-serve situation at the large department store, I didn't feel like I was inconveniencing anyone. (I even returned the garments back to their racks!)

Browse the Shops Virtually

Window shopping the virtual retail scene is a great technique to gather information on brands and styles that interest you. Spending some time perusing the season's new arrivals is a good idea, even if you are a die-hard second-hand shopper. Once you spot something you like, set it on the back burner and practice your patience. This is often where I come up with additions to my preloved wish list.

I've learned that given time, pretty much *everything* ends up on the second-hand market. Classic pieces in particular will stand the test of time and won't leave you looking or feeling dated. You might have to wait until next season (or longer), but that awesome Rag & Bone peacoat with timeless styling and edgy leather trim will eventually be cast away from someone's closet. When the time comes, you will be able to snatch it up for a steal instead of $800. Someone else's wardrobe fail will become your wardrobe win. In this case, the early bird does *not* get the worm!

My advice is, do your research and exercise your patience. Whenever I'm virtually window shopping my favorite brands, I once again make sure to record the specific details of the items that catch my eye (style name and #, price and color). I did in fact snag the Rag & Bone "Battle" peacoat myself for a mere $80. It can only be described as peacoat perfection!

STYLISH SECRETS

- Power up your preloved shopping efforts by gathering some preliminary knowledge that will save you both time and money.

- Maintain a record of your body's measurements so you can compare them to manufacturer size charts and garment details provided by online sellers.

- Collecting brand-specific research will help streamline the preloved shopping process. Identify a list of those brands that suit your style, budget and quality standards.

- If you feel lost when it comes to identifying brands, seek out visual inspiration. Check out your favorite celebrities, bloggers and fashion YouTubers. Make note of those brands that appeal to you.

- Adopt a curious mindset throughout your day. Keep your eyes peeled for well-dressed, stylish people. Don't be shy to pay someone a compliment and ask them where they picked up their fabulous piece!

- Dig into your own closet and identify brands and styles you are happy with. When it comes time to replace or duplicate, draw on the knowledge of your past fashion successes.

- When possible, explore shops in person. Spend some time trying things on to determine your proper size. Use your hands and eyes to assess the quality of the fabric and construction. Make notes on the styles and colorways you are attracted to.

- Visit shops virtually. Window shop the new arrivals and make note of pieces you would like to pick up on the preloved market in the future. The more details you record, the better your chances of sleuthing down a coveted piece.

5

SHOP STRATEGICALLY

I wasn't always a smart and savvy shopper. In fact, for the early part of my adult life, I despised shopping for clothes and avoided it as much as possible. It's human nature to avoid things that make us feel scared and uncomfortable. Shopping for clothes ticked off both of these boxes for me.

Trips to the mall were always last minute and stress inducing! Scared to make my own style choices (mistakes), I relied on the *mannequin mindset*. I purchased my outfits straight off the mannequin. I deduced that someone more stylish than me had compiled the ensemble, so surely it was better than anything I might come up with on my own. This resulted in buying clothes that just didn't feel like me (they could be accurately described as costumes), and therefore ended up gathering dust in the back of my closet.

Online shopping wasn't much better. I was completely overwhelmed by the sheer volume of selection and I wasn't confident in my ability to assess the suitability of a piece based on the photos and descriptions.

Eventually, I learned that I didn't need to be a fashionista in order to assemble a wardrobe that aligned with my personal style and felt fabulous to wear. Like anything in life, you *get out* what you *put in*. Wardrobe planning and shopping is no exception. (Again, I get into great detail on these topics in my book, *Elevate Your Personal Style.*) When it comes to tackling these tasks through preloved fashion, having an effective set of shopping strategies is especially important. The tricks and tactics offered in this chapter will help focus your hunt and assist you in making informed purchase decisions.

Create a Hit List

Arm yourself with a list! This is my number one piece of advice, no matter what you are shopping for. Think back to the last time you hit the grocery store to pick up a few things. Having a well-planned list can make all the difference between coming home with exactly what you need to cook dinner, versus coming home *without* that key ingredient, and a load full of impulse buys (usually junk food!)

Having a hit list of items you are searching for will help keep you focused and on budget. Temptations are everywhere, but they can be particularly sneaky and dangerous when navigating the waters of the preloved market. It's easy to get swept away by jaw-dropping deals. Avoid buying pieces just because they represent an incredible deal. If it doesn't fit into your budget, style and wardrobe plan, then take a pass!

Every few months, I pull out my style journal and create a wardrobe plan for the upcoming season. Taking stock of what I already own, and creating a vision for the new season, allows me to identify the items to be included on my hit list. While compiling the list, I draw heavily on the research I discussed in the previous chapter. In addition to my current wardrobe needs, I also maintain a list of certain long-term treasure pieces I'm hunting for. These are items that I'm willing to pull the trigger on whenever they magically appear. (I've waited years for certain items.)

Your hit list helps to streamline the shopping process, whether you choose to carry it out online or in person. Roaming through a consignment store can feel overwhelming. With your list in hand, you can focus your search through the racks more efficiently. You can also ask the sales associate for assistance in finding a certain piece.

The digital marketplace is vast, so when it comes to shopping for preloved clothing online, a list is an absolute necessity. The more detailed your list, the better your chances of tracking down each particular item. Knowing the names of the style and colorway used by the manufacturer makes searching on some sites much easier.

Shop In Person When Possible

Shopping in person at consignment and thrift stores allows you to examine items closely with your hands, eyes and nose. (As gross as it sounds, a solid sniff of the armpit area is always a good idea!) Getting up close and personal with a garment is the best case scenario when assessing a purchase decision.

Hunt With Laser Focus

The amount of online vs in person shopping you do will largely depend on your location and lifestyle. Most of my second-hand purchases are acquired through online platforms. My personal brand preferences and geographic coordinates make it a necessity.

There are two main approaches to virtually hunting down that yearned for item on your hit list. The first is to *search* for it specifically. The second is to *filter* out the fluff, and narrow in on the prize.

Search Inside and Outside the Box

When it comes to shopping for preloved fashion online, keywords are critical! This is where you really get to put that research into action. If I'm on the hunt for a very specific piece, I begin my pursuit by including as many details as possible in the search bar. I usually start with Google to see where it leads me, or I go directly to a digital preloved shopping platform.

Let's circle back to my cashmere sweater example and take a look at how I would approach seeking out this item. Since I know the brand, style, colorway and size I want, I'd first try typing "Equipment cashmere Sloane peacoat small" into the search bar. If nothing popped up that suited, I'd take the detail down a notch. My next search might be "Equipment cashmere sweater navy small". This search would probably produce a list of turtlenecks, crewnecks, v-necks and anything with a splash of navy in it...but the results should be narrow enough that they are not over-whelming. Chances are, some sellers might not have used the colorway "peacoat" in their description.

It also pays to get creative and search outside the box. This contradicts my previous advice to be detailed and focused, but the truth is, a multi-faceted approach is what works best. Go ahead and throw out the dictionary and deliberately misspell brand names! I have a friend who snagged a wonderful pair of Frye boots on eBay (the very ones worn by Katniss in the Hunger Games), simply because the seller listed them under "Fry". They were missed by regular keyword searches, and her creative approach paid off!

Filter and Find

Pretty much all the preloved fashion sites I've en-countered offer filtering capabilities. This certainly sim-plifies the shopping process, and helps you narrow in on exactly what you are looking for. Sites such as The RealReal don't often include the manufacturer style and colorways in the item descriptions, so using the filter function is a must.

For instance, I was recently on the hunt for the "Aruna Silk Heart Print Sleeveless Blouse" by Joie. I began my search by entering "Joie" in the The RealReal's search bar. I narrowed the search down by selecting the following filters: XS> women> clothing> tops> sleeveless> black. These filter options produced approximately fifty results, which was a manageable number to sift through. I had no problem spotting the sweet heart-printed blouse on my list.

As you familiarize yourself with the different shopping platforms, you will get to know which approach works best in each different scenario.

Get Notified

Life is hectic! With so many commitments and responsibilities competing for our attention, most people are looking for ways to free up time and focus on the more important things in life (i.e., family, friends, hobbies, health). I don't know of anyone who is actually trying to *increase* the amount of time they spend on their devices!

When it comes to shopping for preloved fashion, why not let technology do a bit of the legwork for you? Once you have that hit list compiled, you can set up automatic searches and notifications on your favorite preloved platforms. Instead of cruising the sites every day, you can sit back and relax while you wait for a notification. Again, the more detailed the description you enter into the search field, the more luck you will have in locating a specific item. For instance, I have an automatic search set up on eBay for the Yosi Samra "Preslie perorated flat" in size 7 in both black and biscotti. This brand went out of business several years ago, but their items are still kicking around. I have faith that one day those shoes will magically pop up in my inbox! (I wore my last pair to death, so I know for certain the size and style suit me perfectly.)

You can also sign yourself up for notifications from your favorite consignment shops. It's fun and rewarding to develop a close relationship with your local business owners. Once they get to know you and your personal style, they can keep an eye out for items you might be interested in. It's worth asking if they can notify you immediately if something from your wish list waltzes through their door. They are usually more than happy to help you with your hunt, as it results in a win-win-win situation (for consignee, consignor and you!)

Read Reviews

With so much information available online, you are almost guaranteed to find a review on any specific item. It's clear that many people like to voice their opinions! I view reviews as a potentially helpful source of information that should be regarded with a healthy dose of skepticism. They can be incredibly useful, but on the flip-side, very misleading.

I mainly rely on reviews for sizing information. It's always important to be aware if a piece you are considering runs small, large or true to size. If I'm seeking out an item second-hand, I still draw on the regular retail websites for information. Even if the item is no longer in stock at a store such as Nordstrom or Revolve, the reviews are often still available. Some sites even prompt reviewers to provide their height, weight and usual size when leaving feedback. For instance, Everlane allows you to filter reviews by height, weight and size. As someone on the shorter end of the vertical spectrum, I really appreciate this feature. Finding a proper fit on pants can be very challenging. For the most accurate assessment on sizing, I usually zero in on reviews posted by people who share my body measurements.

Online reviews by bloggers and YouTubers can also provide insight on brands and styles. I have found some to be helpful, but I also take them with a grain of salt. This is especially the case whenever I notice a ton of affiliated links sprinkled throughout an influencer's profile! Sponsored content is everywhere these days, so it's important to read the fine print and maintain a skeptical mindset.

When shopping directly from preloved sellers on sites such as eBay or Poshmark, it's essential to scan the reviews from past customers. Several negative reviews can certainly be a red flag! That being said, I don't immediately discount someone just because they have a bad review next to their name. I drill into the detail to get a better understanding of the issue and how the seller responded.

Don't be Shy to Ask Questions

Being able to communicate directly with the seller is a huge advantage when shopping second-hand. I prefer to shop on sites where I can feed my curiosity by asking questions! Don't be shy to request additional photos or measurements to help in making a final purchase decision.

Because sizing is typically the highest risk area, I often ask sellers for their personal impression of a garment. Does it come from their own closet? In their opinion, does it run small, large or true to size? What size do they normally wear in this brand and others? How did the length suit their height? I've found that most sellers are more than willing to share their honest opinions, as they genuinely want a sales transaction that is successful on both ends. Happy buyers lead to good reviews!

Pull Out the Measuring Tape

When assessing the fit of a potential purchase, my first course of action is to refer to the brand's website. In most cases, manufacturer size charts are helpful and accurate. I also rely on any past experience with the brand. All that brand specific research I discussed in the previous chapter will definitely come in handy when choosing your size. That being said, it's still wise to double check the measurements of the specific garment in question. I often compare the measurements provided in the item description with a piece from my current wardrobe. For instance, if I'm eyeing a shirt, I will compare the pit to pit, shoulder, sleeve and overall length measurements to an item in my closet. If the numbers are a close match, I can feel confident the fit will suit. I've relied on this approach when purchasing shoes, comparing the insole and outer sole measurements with items in my footwear collection.

As you become better acquainted with a number of brands, you may start to identify a few that fall into what I refer to as the high-risk category. I've learned over time that certain brands might produce fabulous clothing, but their sizing is unpredictable and inconsistent. This makes purchasing them second-hand, and in particular online, more tricky.

I'm a huge fan of the Canadian brand Smythe. They create the most amazing jackets, but sadly they hold a spot on my high-risk list. I've been burned a few times with online purchases that were non-refundable. I once purchased a navy "Duchess Blazer" (famously worn by, and subsequently named after, Kate Middleton). I already owned one of their jackets in size 2, so assumed I'd be safe sizing up to a 4. Wrong! It was uncomfortably tight and just didn't suit. Smythe's sizing is all over the map. I own a couple of their pieces in size 2, one in a 4 and one in size 8!

Frye is another brand I've had issues with. I'm normally a 7.5 in footwear, but I've worn everything from a 6.5 to an 8 in their boots.

When it comes to risky brands, I tend to stick to in person shopping. If I choose the online route, I'm extremely careful and thorough in analyzing measurements.

Zoom in on the Details

The condition of preloved clothing can range from pristine to heavily worn. When shopping online specifically, it can be difficult to assess the condition of a piece. It's usually a safe bet when items are described as new with tags (NWT), or new without tags (NWOT). Sellers typically reveal the amount of wear on a garment by disclosing any flaws or stains in the item description and corresponding photographs. Be sure to read all item descriptions in full before clicking buy! Examine all photos carefully by zooming in and assessing each piece with an eagle eye.

View from a Different Angle

When purchasing an item online, it's helpful to view the piece from all angles! At times, the photos provided by the seller might make it difficult to get a good feel for the fit, color and cut of a garment. (I'm not criticizing anyone out there, as my own photography skills are definitely lacking.)

I always make an effort to seek out additional images on the web, so that I can view the piece from different perspectives. For instance, one image might display a blouse tucked in. Another might have it styled untucked, allowing you to assess the length. Online retailers often provide the size of the garment being modelled in their photos, along with the model's measurements. This information is very helpful when assessing fit.

Seeking out additional images is an extra step that, once again, improves the chances that the item will meet your expectations when it arrives on your doorstep.

STYLISH SECRETS

- Shop with a list! Having a wish list helps keep you on track and focused. It allows you to search for items more efficiently by steering you in the right direction (and thereby steering you away from temptation).
- It's always preferable to shop in person when possible. Being able to see, feel, smell and try on garments is the ideal scenario.

- Figure out what keywords will best serve you when searching for a piece online. Begin by entering detailed descriptions in the search bar. If you don't have any luck with this approach, move on to incrementally more generic terms.
- Search using common misspellings for your favorite brands. You might be rewarded for exploring outside the box.
- The use of filters is more effective on some shopping platforms. They allow you to drill down and eliminate the clutter.
- Invest some time in setting up automatic searches and notifications for items on your hit list. This will reduce the amount of time you need to spend online.
- Read product reviews on traditional retail sites to help you assess the sizing and quality of a particular piece.
- A low seller rating is definitely a red flag.
- Be sure to read the seller reviews before clicking buy. Decide for yourself whether you think the seller is trustworthy.
- Sites that allow you to communicate directly with the seller and ask questions are ideal. Don't be shy to request additional photos or measurements if they would assist with your purchase decision.

- In order to assess fit, compare the garment measurements provided in the description with those of a similar item in your wardrobe.

- Certain brands are known for inconsistent and unpredictable sizing. It's best to avoid shopping for these brands online, unless the return policy is flexible and generous. Stick to in person shopping, or take very careful measurements for these particular brands.

- Carefully examine photos for signs of wear or damage. Zoom in for a magnified view!

- Sometimes the photos provided by sellers aren't the most informative. Perform an image search of the item in question in order to capture the view from all angles.

6

DIVE INTO MONEY MATTERS

As an accountant, I'm naturally drawn to money matters, so it's only fitting that I devoted a chapter to this topic. One of the primary benefits of shopping second-hand is saving money!

We've all heard the age-old adage that a vehicle loses 30% of its value as soon as you drive it off the lot. While I suspect this is a guesstimate, there is definitely truth to the notion that preowned goods come with a discounted price tag.

Unlike vehicles, there is no official black or blue book price list published for preloved apparel. How then can you determine if the aftermarket price is fair and reasonable?

Research the Retail Price

I already touched on this in chapter 4, but it's worth revisiting here. Being aware of the retail cost of an item allows you to determine if the resale price is reasonable.

Be sure to check out a few different sites or stores as, depending on the time of the year, it might actually be on sale. I've encountered instances where the second-hand price was higher than the cost of a brand new one!

Research the Preloved Price

It's important to investigate the preloved market value of an item you are considering purchasing. What has this exact item sold for in the past? (Most sites provide access to this historical information.) What is the list price for the same or a similar piece through other sellers? How does the condition of the item impact the price? I'll often sort my search results from lowest to highest before I start digging into the detailed descriptions. My experience is that the preloved price is usually 25-40% of full retail.

If I'm shopping in person at a consignment store, I do a quick price check in the dressing room to make sure it falls in a reasonable zone.

Don't be Afraid to Negotiate

Preloved fashion definitely shares one thing in common with used cars—the price is often not as it first appears! I'm not a haggler by nature, but the culture of the second-hand market is such that many sellers are usually willing to negotiate on price. I learned this early on in my twenties when I started collecting antiques to furnish my home. Before committing to a purchase, I always pulled out the line, "What's your best price for this?" I was rewarded with a discount 99.9% of the time.

In many instances, sellers *expect* to negotiate, and usually set their original price with this in mind. You will often see the "make offer" button available on eBay listings. Poshmark is set up so that the opportunity to "make an offer" is enabled on all listings. Never pass up an opportunity to propose a lower price. The worst that can happen is that the seller declines it, or counteroffers. My experience is that most sellers are willing to knock 10-20% off the list price. If you are an experienced haggler, you might be able to do better than this!

Go With Your Gut

Ultimately, the price you are willing to pay for a preloved piece will be determined by your own gut feeling. We all place value on different things. What I may be willing to pay for an item could vary significantly from what the next person would dole out.

I often fall back on the question, "What's this worth to *me*?" How much do I love this item? How well does it work with the rest of my wardrobe? Is this something I can see myself enjoying for many years to come? Does it align with both my style goals and my budget? Will I need to alter it and if so, how much might this cost? I take all these subjective factors into consideration when determining how much I'm willing to pay for something.

I recently started searching for a pair of vintage 501 Levi's. I was shocked by the wide gap in prices, ranging from $30 to over $200. (The most expensive pair on eBay at the time of writing this book was over $26,000!) Vintage pieces can be particularly tricky to value, as they are often one-of-a-kind. In these instances, the gut approach comes in handy. I've decided the right pair is probably worth about $80 to me. (Obviously other people value an awesome pair of jeans more than I do!)

Be Aware of Hidden Costs

Have you ever purchased an item online for what felt like a reasonable price, only to be stung by a hefty charge at delivery for unexpected brokerage fees, duties and taxes? As a Canadian, I've been burned by unforeseen charges a number of times when ordering from the US and Europe. If you are purchasing an item from a foreign country, be aware that additional charges may apply. Make sure you calculate the door-to-door price before finalizing a purchase.

Double Check the Return Policy

Return policies for preloved goods are usually not as flexible and accommodating as those offered by traditional retailers. A free shipping and returns policy is not the industry norm as it is with many of the large retailers of new clothing. This is why it's so important to feel comfortable with a purchase before handing over your hard-earned money.

If the seller does not permit returns, you will need to decide if it is worth the risk. You will want to take the dollar value of the item into consideration, as well as whether it is resaleable. The odd time I've purchased an item that didn't fit, I was usually able to recoup my losses by turning around and selling it on the preloved market. Occasionally I've even come out further ahead by selling it for more than I paid!

Beware of Unrealistic Prices

It's sad to say, but the production and sale of fake designer goods is a huge (and illegal) industry. When it comes to some of the higher-end pieces, there is definitely a risk of being scammed.

Most consignment stores go to great pains to ensure they only offer authentic merchandise. Some online retailers provide authenticity guarantees. Other platforms charge a fee for authentication services. If you are about to drop a large sum of cash on an item, I recommend you do your homework to assess what safeguards are in place.

Sadly, I speak from experience on this topic. I'll start out by saying that it's usually a red flag if the price is just too good to be true! One of my teenage sons is interested in fashion and style. This past Christmas, I decided to surprise him with a hoodie from one of his favorite brands, Supreme. These things retail for over $300. This was *not* an option, so this savvy Santa decided to shop the preloved market. In no time, I found a hoodie on eBay for a reasonable $25 (NWT). The seller's reviews were good, and everything looked legitimate, so in a moment of naivety, I hastily clicked buy.

I had a nagging feeling something wasn't quite right, so I dug a little deeper into the item description. I realized the hoodie I purchased was actually made by "Supreme Italia", and not the original Supreme brand. It's a knock-off brand that managed to skirt copyright laws to use the Supreme logo. (It's a long, complicated story.)

By the time I figured this out, it was too late to cancel or return the purchase. Needless to say, my brand-conscious son spotted the counterfeit product immediately. Although he appreciated my thoughtfulness, he politely declined the gift! The hoodie fits me, so it's now part of my workout wear. I chalked it all up to a learning experience. I'm embarrassed by my own foolishness, but I hope you learn from my mistakes!

Save on Off-Season Finds

Since you've made it this far through my book, you've probably gathered that I'm a big planner! When it comes to my wardrobe, my head is usually a season or two ahead. Shopping off-season is a great way to snag even better deals on those preloved beauties! If you are in the market for a new pair of winter boots, it is likely the pricing will be more attractive during the warm months when demand is low. This is where that hit list you created will come in handy.

STYLISH SECRETS

- Price is an important factor to consider as it can often make or break a deal. It's therefore essential to know whether the price of a preloved piece is fair and reasonable.

- Research the retail price of the item. What is it currently selling for? Is it on sale? It's not difficult to find out the original price of discontinued and out-of-stock items.

- Research the price of an item on the preloved market. Is it available on another site or from another seller for a different price? What did the same or similar item sell for in the past?

- Never pass up an opportunity to negotiate a lower price. If the make an offer button is available, it is likely the seller is willing to accept less than the listed price.

- One-of-a-kind items can be particularly difficult to value. Rely on your gut and ask yourself the question, "Is this worth it to me?" Take into consideration how much you love the item, whether you foresee enjoying it for years to come, and whether the price fits into your budget.

- Beware of hidden costs and be sure to include them in your estimation of the final price of a piece. Brokerage fees, duties and taxes can be sneaky and shockingly high!

- The return policies on preowned goods are usually not as flexible and accommodating as you might be used to. If returns are not permitted, or if you will be responsible for return fees, consider whether the purchase is worth the risk.

- No one likes being scammed! You will want to feel comfortable that the item you are purchasing is legitimate. Many sellers offer authentication services for higher-end pieces. If the price is too good to be true, it just might be!

- Buying clothes out of season is a great way to save on price. Plan ahead and keep your hit list handy. Try thinking and shopping a full season ahead to maximize on the opportunity to snag some deals.

7

LET GO OF PERFECTIONISM

If you were a child of the eighties like me, you may have been a fan of the coming-of-age movie, *Pretty in Pink* starring Molly Ringwald. (If you haven't seen it, skip this paragraph and go watch it. It's a classic!) I love the sewing scene where Andie designs and creates her famous pink prom dress. She fashioned it by deconstructing two other dresses: a friend's vintage polka dot number, and one given to her by her dad. Opinions are divided on this famous dress. (Apparently Molly Ringwald hated it so much she burst into tears when she first laid eyes on it.) Whether you liked it or not, it definitely suited the main character's eclectic new-wave style.

Andie's attitude and approach to personal style is inspiring! She was able to see the potential in both dresses, transforming them into her personal version of prom perfection. Although most of us likely don't share Andie's sewing skills (yay for you if you do!), we can assume a similar, open-minded approach when evaluating a garment.

Adopting a less rigid outlook on life is something I've been working on, especially since I became a mother! (A motto I'm increasingly relying on is, "It's good enough.") As a recovering perfectionist, I encourage you to consider relaxing your standards when assessing preloved items. Honing your ability to visualize the potential of an imperfect piece can result into truly fabulous finds.

Flaws and fit issues are not always dealbreakers. Oftentimes, it's worth exploring the possibilities of repairing and/or reworking a piece to make it your own. In fact, items with minor defects are often heavily discounted, so they represent wonderful opportunities.

There are many options when it comes to tweaking preloved pieces to suit your needs. Some are easy fixes, and some require calling in an expert! Gaining knowledge of the various repair and alteration options is a great place to start. This will allow you to evaluate potential purchases with an informed approach.

Do It Yourself

I'm not a skilled seamstress or cobbler, but I do have a few simple tricks up my sleeve! I rely on these quick, easy and inexpensive fixes regularly to fine-tune my fashion finds.

As I mentioned earlier, my mother sewed most of my clothing growing up. Sadly, I didn't inherit the sewing gene. I am dreadful with a needle and thread. I have managed to hack together a few simple projects around the house (pillow cases and curtains), but I would never attempt to alter (ruin) a garment of my own. I *can*, however, sew on a button!

It's not uncommon for preloved items to be missing the odd button. These "flawed" pieces usually come with a nice discount. A trip to your local fabric or craft store will usually supply you with anything you need. If it is a hard-to-find item, you can likely locate a close match at an online button speciality store. (The selection is astounding.)

I purchased a beautiful preloved Emerson Fry coat that was missing a decorative button on one of the epaulettes. I discovered an almost perfect match online, and the coat is as good as new. In an effort to soften the prim and proper vibe of a blazer, I once replaced a set of shiny gold buttons with some vintage ones I picked up on Etsy. I also switched out the plastic buttons on a wool camel coat with horn ones to give it a more luxe look. (Yes, I have a lot of coats. I live in Canada and I'm always cold! They get *a lot* of use.)

At 5'3", I rarely come across a pair of pants that doesn't need hemming. I have a wonderful tailor who I usually entrust with this task. On a couple of occasions, I've taken the do-it-yourself approach with my jeans. While I'm not a big fan of heavy distressing, I love the look of a rough-cut hem. All you need is a good pair of scissors, a measuring tape and the guts to do it. After a couple of runs through the wash, they will be perfectly imperfect!

Oftentimes, the flaws are purely cosmetic, and the piece just needs a little pick me up. A run over with the lint brush, or a press of the iron is all that is required to breathe new life into a garment. Stains can be a little tricky to assess, as it's likely they have been sitting in the fabric for quite some time. Examine a stain carefully to determine if you think it can be removed. If a blemish is located in an inconspicuous spot, it's really a non-issue. Certain stains, such as white deodorant marks left behind from a try-on, are really quite easy to get out. (This probably goes without saying, but avoid yellow sweat stains!)

When it comes to preloved footwear, I tend to stay away from anything that is heavily worn. Over time, shoes mold to the shape of our feet, so I much prefer to be the one doing the breaking in! Most preloved shoes or boots I've purchased were only worn a couple of times. A quick rub of shoe polish is all that is needed to buff out any superficial marks or scratches.

Footwear is difficult to purchase on the preloved market. Shoes purchased online are risky from a fit perspective, especially when there is a no-return policy in place. Every now and then I end up purchasing a pair of shoes that is a less-than-perfect fit. I've used insoles and heel cushions to make shoes a little more snug. I also own a simple shoe stretcher I picked up on Amazon. While it certainly can't work miracles, it has done the trick on a few tight spots.

I keep a fashion toolkit handy for all my do-it-yourself fixes. Have fun stocking your own kit with all the essentials. It might include a sewing kit, de-fuzzing tool, measuring tape, sharp scissors, lint brush, stain remover, shoe polish, shoe stretcher, padded insoles, heel lifts, and unique buttons.

Visit the Tailor

For more complicated repairs and alternations, I call on the experts. I have an amazing tailor who does impeccable work. I always feel confident that I'm leaving my precious pieces in good hands. He's been part of my personal style team for a number of years, so he knows exactly how I like my clothes to fit.

When it comes to alterations and repairs, the more complex the job, the more it is going to cost you. It is therefore important to be able to differentiate between simple and complicated solutions, so you can decide if they are worth your while.

The bulk of my tailoring jobs involve shortening. It is not uncommon for me to need pants, skirts and dresses hemmed four inches. This is a fairly simple fix in most cases, so the cost is usually very reasonable. I rarely pass up on a piece because of length. Coats, however, can be a bit tricky. Shortening a lined coat is a more involved alternation, so the price for tailoring reflects this. Anything that involves moving sleeve cuffs or adjusting shoulders is going to be expensive.

Your best bet is to speak with a tailor. Explain your issue and find out if it is something that can be fixed. Be sure to get a quote and factor this figure into the final price of the piece before you make your purchase decision.

Visit the Cobbler

The popularity of athletic footwear and cheap throwaway shoes has made it tough for those working in the shoe repair business! While cobblers may be a dying (or perhaps evolving) breed, they offer so many fabulous services. Many people never think to repair or alter their shoes, but it is a marvelous option for extending the life of a much-loved pair, or finetuning any footwear that is less than perfect.

As I mentioned, when it comes to preloved footwear, I tend to stick to items that are in new or nearly-new condition. That being said, you may encounter a stunning pair of used shoes that just needs a bit of TLC. I've seen cobblers perform some pretty magical transformations, so keep the option of shoe repair in your back pocket when assessing preloved footwear. I usually call on the services of a cobbler when my heavily-worn shoes are in need of a makeover. It's definitely worth the money to have high-quality footwear repaired, resoled or reheeled.

Cobblers offer a variety of services that you may not have considered. If you find yourself stuck with a snug fit and a no-return policy, a trip to the cobbler may save the day. Cobblers have much better stretching tools and methods than the do-it-yourself options.

Do you have any leather goods that just don't suit your color scheme? I once purchased a preowned brown leather belt that turned out to be more orange than I was expecting. I brought it into the shoe repair shop, and they dyed it a beautiful deep, rich brown for very little cost. I also had a small red Longchamp bag transformed into a deeper cranberry shade.

Cobblers can also help out with fast, inexpensive and easy fixes to your favorite leather goods. They can punch an extra hole in your belt, and shorten the straps on that handbag!

As with the tailor, it's a good idea to get a quote on alterations if you are contemplating a purchase that needs a few tweaks.

What's it Worth?

When deciding whether to invest in a repair or alternation, it's once again helpful to rely on your gut instincts.

I like to come back to the question I mentioned in the last chapter, "Is this worth it to me?" If you are in love with a deficient item that holds great potential, the financial cost may very well be *worth it to you*!

I purchased a stunning Isabel Marant coat on eBay several years ago. (Yes, another coat example!) I wasn't familiar with the brand at the time, but the seller allowed returns, so I decided to take the risk. When I opened the parcel, I was disappointed to discover it had an awkward set of shoulder pads that wasn't apparent in the photographs. I have broad shoulders to begin with, so I like to avoid extra bulk in that area. It was obvious they could be removed, but the shoulders would have to be reworked to remove the excess fabric. To make matters more complicated, the coat was striped, so lining things up could be tricky. Instead of heading to the post office for a return, I took a detour to the tailor shop. He admired the quality of the coat and was genuinely excited to help me out. His quote was high due to the complex nature of the alteration, but I was confident he'd work his magic. The price he charged was *worth it to me*. At the end of the day, I have a unique, high-quality piece that fits me perfectly and has been a wardrobe favorite for nearly a decade.

STYLISH SECRETS

- Evaluate potential preloved purchases with an open mind. Even items with small flaws can hold great potential. A little problem solving can go a long way in perfecting a piece.

- Get acquainted with the available options for repair and alteration. This will allow you to make informed decisions when assessing a damaged, flawed or ill-fitting item.

- Many fixes are easy and inexpensive to deal with on your own. Have fun creating your own fashion tool-kit that will allow you to perform quick makeovers.

- Find a good tailor you can trust! Get to know the difference between simple and complicated alterna-tions. Be sure to ask for a quote and include this in the final price of the garment.

- Get acquainted with the services offered by your local cobbler, as well as the related costs. They often extend beyond basic shoe repair. A good dye job can breathe new life into tired-looking leather. Shortening the strap on your favorite handbag can make a world of difference!

- When evaluating a repair or alteration quote, check in with your gut. Only you will know if the price is *worth it*. If you truly love the piece and foresee enjoying it for many years to come, it's likely worth the cost and effort.

8

START SMALL

I've armed you with a lot of information so far, which might take time to digest. It can feel scary to dive into a new adventure head first! If the idea of preloved fashion is new to you, I suggest you test the waters of the second-hand clothing market by dipping your toe in the kiddie end of the pool! If you are feeling a bit unsure or apprehensive, this makes the whole experience a little easier on both the head and the heart.

I want your first experience with preloved goods to be a positive, pleasant and rewarding one. Starting out using a gentle and thoughtful approach sets you up for success! Feeling good about your first trial run will leave a satisfying taste in your mouth. You will want to come back for more, and in turn, enjoy further opportunities to save money, consume in a more sustainable manner, and elevate your style!

I'm going to walk through some easy and approachable strategies to get you started on your second-hand fashion journey. It's a good idea to have your style journal on hand to jot down notes and ideas as they pop into your head. These scribblings can serve as a launch pad when you take off into preloved shopping action!

Adopt a Balanced Mindset

I've lost track of the number of times I've been revved up and inspired about a new project, only to sabotage my efforts with a set of strict, ridiculous and unattainable rules. Although we are often encouraged to, "go big or go home", this approach often leaves me feeling over-whelmed and stressed (and set up for failure).

When my first son was around two years old, the media exploded with controversy surrounding the use of bisphenol A (BPA) in food containers. I was bombarded with alarming news articles about the potential health risks associated with exposure to this chemical, particularly for children. When I realized that our family's brand of baby bottles was considered toxic, my mama-bear instincts kicked in! Feeling disappointed, frightened and angry, I embarked on a mission to *remove all plastic* from my children's lives. (You can probably already guess how this story ends.)

Obviously, my first move was to trash the offending baby bottles and switch to glass. From there, I went on a rampage, that started (but did not end) in the kitchen. I replaced all the plastic food storage containers with glass, traded in my plastic measuring cups for stainless steel, swapped out my plastic mixing spoons with wood, started buying ketchup in glass bottles, sewed fabric snack bags to avoid plastic baggies…etc. I even secretly shipped all of my kids' plastic toys to the goodwill shop. (This last one may have scarred them for life. I did feel a pang of guilt when my son innocently inquired why half the toy box mysteriously disappeared). I won't bore you any further with my extensive and expensive list of plastic eliminating measures!

Living a life completely free of plastic became a daunting and exhausting endeavor, but I was committed…until the day I wasn't. This was the day I proudly proclaimed to my husband that I had finally achieved success! I no longer had to worry about exposing my children to potential toxic chemicals, because 99.99% of their food containers and toys were plastic-free! He responded with the following statement, "Jen, you do realize all the water pipes in our house are made of plastic?"

What could I do at this point but laugh at my neurotic self? I realized, it wasn't all or nothing. I could do my best to keep our family safe and healthy, without living by an impossible set of self-imposed standards. I didn't throw in the towel completely, but decided to take a more balanced and strategic approach to my plastic-free policy. Although I stuck to the glass baby bottles, I did allow plastic baggies, among other conveniences, to creep back into my life. (The kids lost all the fabric ones I had painstakingly crafted anyway!)

What does this story have to do with the topic of shopping for second-hand fashion? It just serves as a reminder to adopt wardrobe and shopping goals that are realistic and achievable! I've learned that life is less stressful and more enjoyable when I limit the list of self-imposed rules I *should* follow. There is no need to burden yourself with ridiculous standards that will only leave you feeling guilty, pressured and deflated!

While I may have convinced you of all the amazing benefits of second-hand shopping, there is no need to adopt an all-or-nothing approach! I admire those people who can stick to a challenge, such as the #nonewclothes movement. Personally, however, I'm always more content when I approach life with a balanced mindset. Although I'm obviously a huge fan of shopping preloved, I don't buy used clothing exclusively. My personal wardrobe is a mix of preloved and brand new, which suits me perfectly.

Last spring, I added a beautiful and practical pair of black pants to my wardrobe. I purchased them directly from a small Canadian designer, Allison Wonderland. Her garments are all made in Canada and are produced in very limited quantities. Allison is extremely kind and is always helpful when it comes to determining proper sizing and fit. She once whipped up a dress on her sewing machine just for me, as it was out of stock in my size! I enjoy supporting her business, as well as small locally owned boutiques. There are also instances where I just reach for the easy solution, and buy from a large retailer.

I pick and choose what I source second-hand carefully based on availability, price and quality. The key is to find an approach that ties in with *your* personal goals, values, budget, lifestyle and style.

Shop In Person

When it comes to shopping for second-hand finds, I use a mixed bag approach. I shop both online and in person at my local consignment shops. If you are new to the preloved market, I recommend you start your journey by visiting one of your local consignment shops. It's a lot less risky than starting out online, because you can see exactly what you are paying for. Being able to touch, examine, sniff and try on a garment before making a purchase decision is always preferrable. Lowering the risk increases the chance you will be happy with your purchase.

The first item I ever purchased at a consignment store was a tan Coach handbag. Being able to hold the bag in my hands and assess its condition (absolutely pristine) with my own senses allowed me to feel very comfortable with my purchase decision. I knew I loved it, and the price was more than reasonable. This small taste of success motivated me to continue treasure hunting.

Limit Financial Risk

Buyer's remorse is no fun, especially when it comes with a hefty price tag. Limit both financial risk and regret by starting out with an inexpensive and easy purchase. This is a fantastic approach if you are feeling uneasy about shopping online.

A pretty and unique scarf is something you can find easily for a very reasonable price. It's also a wardrobe piece that can have a powerful impact on elevating an outfit from plain to extraordinary. I've purchased vintage silk scarves on Etsy for as low $7. Inexpensive accessories of any kind are definitely a great starting point for rookies.

Use the Perfect-Fit Strategy

Another strategy for ensuring a positive purchasing experience is to seek out items where size truly doesn't matter. The handbag and scarf purchases I mentioned previously are perfect examples of pieces that provide a *perfect fit*, no matter your shape or body size.

A friend of mine recently made her first aftermarket fashion purchase on eBay. She decided to try her hand at second-hand shopping after reading my book, *Elevate Your Personal Style*. I had piqued her interest, but she was still feeling a little unsure and apprehensive. She opted for the perfect-fit strategy by seeking out a classic Burberry cashmere scarf. These timeless beauties will easily set you back $500 at full retail. Her preloved scarf landed on her doorstep in mint condition for $100. She admitted there was a point she was actually going to fork over the funds for a brand new version. She is so glad she placed the purchase on the back burner and revisited her shopping strategy. Again, you don't have to be an accountant to appreciate and celebrate such significant savings!

The whole idea is to set yourself up for success. Have fun exploring and investigating all the options where the perfect fit strategy is a *perfect fit*! Scarves, handbags, earrings, necklaces, wrist watches, wallets and sunglasses all make great starter purchases.

Choose a Slam Dunk

Great success and savings are up for grabs when you opt for a slam-dunk purchase. When it comes to clothing, it's not one size fits all. Size matters! I decided to use the slam-dunk approach by purchasing something I already owned and loved. I sought out my favorite style of jeans in a different color wash. I already knew the brand, size and style, so it was an easy, no-risk purchase.

Do you have any items in your current wardrobe that need to be replaced or that you would like multiples of? Duplicates make perfect starter pieces for rookie shoppers.

Seek Out Pristine Items

The terms second-hand and preloved are a little misleading. They tend to conjure up images of items that are worn out, shabby or dingy. Unless you are in search of authentically distressed denim as I once was, you probably aren't looking to add a bunch of scruffy clothing into your existing wardrobe.

Once you start digging into the resale market, you will quickly realize that there are many items up for offer that are in pristine condition. I have very high standards for anything I bring into to my closet, and I assure you, there are magnificent treasures out there, just waiting to be discovered. The truth is, a lot of what is available is brand new, or nearly new. It's not uncommon to find garments with the tags still attached! Think of all those items you purchased over the years that hung in your closet lonely and neglected. These are the types of goods that end up for sale on the aftermarket! One woman's fashion mistake becomes another woman's fashion score!

If you are feeling icky or nervous about buying something that has been previously worn, ease yourself into the preloved market. Seek out items that are specifically identified as brand new. This is an easy strategy to use for online shopping. Most of the virtual preloved platforms allow you to filter your searches to only include new items. When searching on a website such as eBay, I use the acronym

NWT (new with tags) or NWOT (new without tags) to refine my hunt.

STYLISH SECRETS

- Make your first second-hand shopping experience a positive and rewarding one. When first starting out, it's wise to opt for shopping strategies that offer the best chance of success. A good deal on a fabulous find will inspire you to continue experiencing the benefits of the preloved fashion market.

- Adopt a balanced and flexible mindset when it comes to building a wardrobe that suits both your personality and your lifestyle. Avoid strict, self-imposed rules that might leave you feeling stressed. There is no need to get extreme and ban all new clothes from your closet (unless that is something you feel passionate about). A wardrobe that includes both new and used items can be sustainable, budget friendly and super chic!

- Shopping at brick-and-mortar consignment stores allows you to inspect an item thoroughly before purchasing it. Buying in person is a great way to dive into the preloved market, as it eliminates some of the uncertainty and risk associated with online shopping.

- Make your fist preloved purchase a fun, but inexpensive one. There are lots of great little starter items available that allow you to whet your appetite for second-hand shopping, while limiting your financial risk. Ideas include a chic vintage scarf, or a cute pair of fashion earrings.

- When shopping online for the first time, ensure a perfect fit by choosing an item where size doesn't matter! Scarves, handbags and most jewelry fall into the one-size-fits-all category.

- Seek out items you already own and love. Buying a duplicate of a current piece in your wardrobe will ensure success as you know exactly what you are getting.

- If you are feeling uneasy about the concept of used clothing, seek out brand new pieces on the aftermarket. It is easy to track down garments that still have the price tags attached!

9

MAKEOVER YOUR MINDSET

Have you had the opportunity to take a dip in the shallow end of the pool? Are you ready to shed your water wings and bravely head into the deep end? Maybe a couple of preloved fashion scores have you feeling inspired and you are ready to kick things up a notch. Small successes at the beginning can be very effective at opening your eyes to the possibility of building almost your *entire* wardrobe with preloved fashion (no pressure of course).

I relied heavily on the starter strategies outlined in chapter 8 when I first forayed into the second-hand fashion scene. After the purchase of that Coach handbag, I continued using the perfect fit approach for quite a while. It definitely felt safe to stick with accessories at the beginning, especially when shopping online. That first winter of my preloved journey, I picked up a gorgeous camel-colored cashmere scarf on eBay. It was by Club Monaco, a brand

I was familiar and comfortable with. I've had it for almost a decade, and I still look forward to wrapping myself up in its coziness every winter.

My success with preloved accessories completely transformed my approach to shopping. I started to realize that practically any item on my wish list could be acquired aftermarket. I was simply going to have to adjust my mindset and my shopping strategies.

Are you ready to get serious about sourcing your clothing on the preloved market and building your dream wardrobe in the process? I've set you up with a set of tips and tricks, but if you are genuinely interested in expanding your horizons and sourcing your attire predominantly second-hand, it will require a deliberate shift in *mindset.*

Adopt a Seek Out Second-Hand First Mindset

Perhaps you are used to shopping on auto-pilot. If you are set in your ways, you'll need to shift your mindset about how, where and when you acquire a new pieces for your wardrobe. I have adopted a little goal for myself. When I need something new, I always investigate the preloved market *first.* I refer to this as the *second-hand first* mindset.

I don't pretend to be a die-hard second-hand shopper. As I've mentioned, my wardrobe is comprised of a mix of new and preloved pieces. Being a bean counter (or rather, jean counter), I couldn't help but head up to my closet to perform an impromptu inventory count on my current season's wardrobe. My rough calculations show that the split is about 74% preloved and 26% new. The spread between these two numbers has definitely grown over the years. Later on in this book, I walk you through a case study of my fall/winter wardrobe additions from this past year. The split comes in at 75% preloved, 25% new. Stay tuned for the details!

Set yourself up for the challenge! Adopt the second-hand first mindset and see where this path leads you. Make the conscious decision to explore the road less travelled. Explore all the fabulous second-hand sources outlined in chapter 3, instead of automatically heading for the big department store (either virtually or in person).

Once you get the hang of sourcing your wardrobe with preloved finds, why not expand your horizons? I encourage you to apply the second-hand first mindset to other purchase decisions in your life—furniture, housewares, toys, tools, building materials, pet supplies…the opportunities are endless! (Yes, even my two little poodles, Coco and Junior, are sporting trendy, preloved canine fashion!)

Adjust Your Expectations

Building a fantastic and functional wardrobe filled with second-hand treasures is very much an achievable goal. Considering the explosion of the preloved fashion market in recent years, it's easier today than ever before.

That being said, travelling down the preloved fashion route will require an adjustment in your expectations. The experience of shopping preowned versus new is going to look and feel a bit different than you are used to. Why not view it as a new and exciting adventure that offers so many more benefits than the status quo?

Let's say you are in need of a new pair of winter boots. How would you normally approach shopping for this key piece in your wardrobe? If you prefer to shop in person, you would likely head straight for the mall or local boutiques to browse this season's offerings. If you are more of an online shopper, you might find yourself scrolling the bookmarked sites of your favorite brands and big department stores. In our consumeristic society, there is no shortage of goods vying for the attention of our hard-earned dollars. My guess is, the selection of winter boots you uncover will be abundant, if not overwhelming. We've all grown accustomed to being offered a staggering number of choices, no matter what we're in the market for. (Am I the only one who finds the selection in the toothpaste isle mind boggling? I actually miss the days when the choice was limited to Crest, Colgate and Aquafresh. The biggest decision back then was paste or gel.)

When you choose to take a detour and travel the preloved route, the destination might look the same (a new pair of boots in the closet), but the path you take to get there, and the scenery it offers along the way, will look a little different (and arguably a bit more interesting!) You may have to grow accustomed to not having quick access to a sizable selection to choose from. In my experience, having a narrower set of choices can be both refreshing and liberating!

Let Go of Last Minute

I am a planner by nature and like to pride myself on being efficient, organized and productive. That being said, like all humans, I have my areas of weakness. When faced with certain dreaded or uncomfortable tasks, I sometimes invite my friend Mrs. Procrastination over for a cup of tea and a serving of avoidance.

Shopping for clothes used to compete with visiting the dentist for the top spot on my list of unpleasant to do's! I always considered it a necessary but evil part of life. If you read my book, *Elevate Your Personal Style,* you know that I struggled for years to gain the confidence and skills to dress myself in a way that truly captured the essence of my personal style. For the first part of my adult life, shopping for clothes was an experience that evoked feelings of fear, angst, frustration and insecurity. When in the market for a new piece of clothing, the old me always hit the mall in an eleventh-hour panic.

During those early years as a stay-at-home mom, trudging around in oversized sweatshirts and yoga pants (or admittedly pajamas), I cringed anytime an invitation to a special event landed in my mailbox. No matter the nature of the event or dress-code, it was pretty much impossible to pull together an appropriate outfit from my dingy, dull and mismatched wardrobe. I'd scurry off to the mall in a frenzy to grab something deemed suitable (or at least not pathetic).

My experience with panic shopping is that it typically leads to buyer's remorse. Most of those last-minute purchases served as single-wear pieces that ended up in the back of my closet, and eventually the donation bin at my local charity shop. (An awful pair of brown velvet pants comes to mind.) My dysfunctional approach resulted in an immense waste of time, money and resources.

I've completely changed my tune since those days of early adulthood. These days, I genuinely enjoy both the creative and practical aspects of planning my wardrobe. I owe my change in attitude to two main factors. Firstly, I immersed myself in a journey of self-discovery that allowed me to gain a clear understanding of my preferences and my true personal style. Secondly, I now have a *plan*! I'm no longer flying by the seat of my pants when it comes to building a cohesive, functional and chic wardrobe. Since I'm always thinking a season or two ahead, I get to stew over my purchase decisions carefully, and give myself plenty of time to track down the items on my wish list (instead of settling on panic purchases as I did in the past). Careful planning has allowed me to slowly build a wardrobe of beautiful, flexible and timeless pieces that I absolutely adore.

When it comes to shopping second-hand, planning ahead is incredibly important! If you normally shop last minute, you may have to adjust your strategy. There will be times where finding that perfect piece will require some digging! Having that working wish list in your style journal will allow you to explore the second-hand market using an unhurried, well-thought-out approach.

Exercise Patience with Creativity

Building a wardrobe from preloved sources can certainly require an extra dose of patience. It goes without saying that patience and planning go hand in hand. This isn't necessarily a bad thing! In fact, waiting for the right piece gives you time to contemplate your decisions carefully instead of constantly rushing out for a hit of instant gratification. As time chugs along, you may realize you don't really want or need that initially coveted item (which of courses provides the extra bonus of saving money).

While waiting for an item on your wish list, you may be forced to exercise some creativity with your current collection of clothing and accessories. Again, this can result in many positives! It's referred to in fashion circles as "shopping your closet". You learn to make do with what you own, and perhaps rediscover pieces in your closet that have been neglected and ignored. If this concept intrigues you, I recommend you check out Alyssa Beltempo's YouTube channel. She is truly an inspiration on the slow-fashion front, and is a master of the shop-your-closet method. (She's also Canadian!) I participated in one of her virtual live shop-your-closet events and plan to sign up for more. Not only are they super fun, but you leave feeling inspired and motivated to become a more creative and conscious consumer.

To illustrate, let's say you are on the lookout for new down-filled winter coat. The thin woolen one you wore the last three seasons is stylish and attractive, but it's just not keeping you toasty enough while you wait at the bus stop! You've got your eye on a luxurious coat by Mackage (my patriotic plug for another awesome Canadian brand), but your budget recoiled at the retail price tag! You have faith your dream coat will someday appear on the preloved scene in your size, and you are willing to wait! In the meantime, you get creative with what you already have hanging in the closet. You try layering your sporty down puffer vest under your wool coat for an extra layer of warmth. While experimenting with this temporary solution, you actually realize you love the look and vibe of this unexpected combination! It's always fun and rewarding to discover new, creative and flexible ways to wear your favorite pieces.

Over the years, I've gotten used to exercising my patience muscles. I've mentioned this before, and it is worth repeating, if you are willing to wait, that highly-coveted item on your wish list *will* eventually turn up!

This summer I finally got my hands on a gorgeous tweed peacoat I've been dreaming about for ages. I spotted this coat by Smythe in a consignment shop five or six years ago. Although I fell in love with it as soon as I slipped it on, I realized that no amount of tailoring was going to take it down to my size. I snapped a photo and tucked it into my long-term wish list. My patience paid off, because it finally popped up on The RealReal for a mere $75. I've mentioned before that Smythe coats run around $700 and beyond, so this is an incredible steal of a deal on a very high-quality, timeless and stylish piece.

Of course, as I've said from the start, preloved shopping is not about suffering and making yourself miserable with rigid rules and unrealistic expectations. It's really about finding a balanced approach to shopping that suits your values, budget and lifestyle. If you urgently need an item in your wardrobe, and the second-hand market is coming up dry, go ahead and source the item when and where necessary!

STYLISH SECRETS

- Once you've tested the waters of the preloved fashion market, you may be inspired to wade deeper! It's definitely possible to source the vast majority of your wardrobe needs second-hand. This new way of shopping, however, will require a shift in mindset.

- Whenever you are in need of a new wardrobe piece, adopt a *second-hand first* mindset. Explore and investigate all the preloved options before opting for brand new.

- Building a wardrobe with preloved finds often involves more planning. It might take some digging to locate an item on your wish list. Embrace the slower pace. Panic shopping often ends in disappointment and remorse!

- Maintaining a style journal, and planning ahead for the upcoming season, will provide you with plenty of time to seek and find the items on your wish list.

- You will likely need to exercise more patience when sourcing your wardrobe on the preloved market. A special piece is always worth the wait.

- Being forced to delay the purchase of an item on your wish list can be beneficial. With more time to contemplate, you may realize that you don't need or want the coveted item. This will save you money in the long run!

- Have fun using your creativity by making do with what is already in your closet! While you continue your search for that special piece, you may discover unique and fun combinations from your current selection that you had not considered.
- Don't make yourself miserable with strict, self-imposed rules. If you can't find what you desperately need on the second-hand market, don't feel guilty about going the traditional retail route. There's no need to adopt all-or-nothing thinking. This is supposed to be fun!

10

CASH IN ON YOUR CASTOFFS

The first year or two of my style journey was a bit bumpy. In the early days, I experienced quite a few style stumbles. Because I didn't have a true sense of my own unique personal style, I spent too much time and money trying to copy others.

I was friends with a very hip, stylish and edgy woman who absolutely rocked the bohemian look. During this period of my life, I drew heavily on the mannequin mindset I described in chapter 5. She essentially became my living mannequin, and I purchased many of the same pieces she owned. Back then, we were both really into the brand Free People. I have nothing against it, and I think their aesthetic looks incredible on a lot of people (my friend being one of them). The whole flowy, bohemian vibe, however, never felt like me.

Perhaps it's human nature to want to play pretend and slip into someone else's shoes. Free People describes their customer as, "a 26-year-old girl, smart, creative, confident and comfortable in all aspects of her being, free and adventurous, sweet to tough to tomboy to romantic. A girl who likes to keep busy and push life to its limits, with traveling and hanging out and everything in between." Wow, who *wouldn't* want to be this girl?

The truth is, I was a stay-at-home mom of two in my mid-thirties who was busy carting around kids, cleaning up spills and doing laundry. There wasn't a lot of time, money or energy available for traveling the world and hanging out with girlfriends! Since one of my sons transformed into a devil child at night, I was running on about four hours of sleep each day. I was definitely pushing myself to the limits, so at least I had that part going for me!

In all honesty, I was genuinely happy with my life back then. I felt fortunate to be in a position where I could spend my days with my two precious babies. (Little devil turned into an angel when the sun rose.) Sure, I recognized that I wanted to start taking better care of myself and upgrade my personal image, but I realized that the changes had to come from within. I had to look inward and connect with my true self. I had to get in touch with the real me, instead of trying to emulate someone else.

So, as you can imagine, I ended up with a closet full of expensive clothes (costumes, rather) in need of rehoming. I'm guessing each and every one of us is guilty of hoarding garments that we've never worn, or never intend to. Everyone makes mistakes. We sometimes buy clothes for a fantasy life that doesn't coincide with our reality. Our circumstances and lifestyles change, and as a result, our wardrobe requirements do as well. We hang on to clothes that no longer fit our changing bodies and our seasons of life. We buy things on impulse, not because we need them, but because they are on sale. Heavy feelings of guilt weigh us down every time we catch sight of these lonesome, unworn garments cluttering up our closets.

It's time to free yourself and face facts. The initial money you spent is gone, and no matter how long you hang on to the items, it isn't coming back. In fact, finding a new home for your castoffs is a wonderful way to mitigate your mistakes, recoup some of your losses, and fund your fashion budget. The sentimental side of me also loves the idea of finding a good, loving home for my castoffs!

Although this book is clearly meant to focus on shopping for preloved fashion, I thought it was worthwhile to provide an introduction and overview of the other side of the equation…selling preloved fashion. Chances are, once you get the hang of sourcing items on the preloved market, you might be inspired to offload any wardrobe rejects in exchange for cash!

There are many options when it comes to selling your unwanted clothing and accessories. Some are simple, and others require a bit more time and effort.

Consign Your Castoffs

By far, the easiest option is to let someone else do all the legwork. Consignment shops provide easy access to the resale market. You can consign using a brick-and-mortar option, or you can go the virtual route. If you decide to use a local consignment store, you simply drop off your items in person (in clean condition of course). Some online platforms, such as The RealReal, will send a courier to your home to pick up your items. Once the shop receives your pieces, they look after the rest—from merchandising to money matters. When your item sells, you receive your share of the prize money. This amount will vary depending on the details of the consignment agreement. Generally, the consignee takes home 30-50% of the sale price. Make sure to thoroughly review the consignment agreement so you know what you are getting into.

Going the consignment route is a great option if you want to keep things as simple as possible. Of course, you will end up with less cash in your pocket, since you are essentially paying the shop a seller's fee. Some shops are very particular about the brands they are willing to take on, so you may need to visit a couple before you find a good match.

I sold all my Free People clothing through my local consignment store. They were apparently hot-ticket items and were snatched up quite quickly. (I guess I wasn't the only one trying to turn myself into a Free People dream girl.) At the time, I was very busy with two small children at home, so I reached for the easiest solution available. Although I could have made more money peddling them myself on eBay, I was happy with the end result.

Take Control of the Reigns

The resale fashion market is exploding in popularity, and as a result, more and more sites are popping up that connect seller to consumer directly. I touched on these in chapter 3. Sites like eBay, Etsy, Poshmark, Tradesy, Depop, Vestiaire Collective and Vinted all fall under this category. These sites provide a platform from which to sell, but you as the seller are responsible for photographing your items, creating product descriptions, negotiating the price, answering buyer questions and shipping the goods.

Another option is to set up shop on your personal social media page. Facebook Marketplace is a popular choice. I belong to a group called *Sézane Addicts USA-Canada*. It's a wonderful space to buy or sell brand-specific pieces.

There are pros and cons to each platform, so if you are interested in taking full ownership for your rehoming efforts, I suggest you do your research and decide which option best suits your situation. Since I live in Canada, for instance, Tradesy is not available to me. Poshmark is, but it limits my sales within the Canadian border. Some sites automatically produce shipping labels for you, while others require you to handle delivery on your own. The fees, of course, vary by site, depending on the level of service that is being provided.

I've personally set up shop on both eBay and Poshmark. My experience with eBay was fine, but lately I have been focusing my efforts on my Poshmark closet (the term they use for your online shop). Although eBay allowed me to ship internationally, I had to handle all the shipping details on my own. Poshmark restricts my market to Canada, but I love that they provide postage labels. The selling process is slick, easy and pretty low maintenance.

Since I've become more comfortable as a seller, I always make a first attempt at selling an item on my own. If I don't have success on Poshmark, I try my luck at a local consignment shop. If that option fails, the garments make their way to the charity donation bin. (On a side note, charitable donation bins are a controversial topic, as reports are surfacing that the bulk of these garments end up clogging up landfills in third-world countries. Lately I have been looking for solutions that ensure my donations find their way back into circulation. This is a topic for another day and another book!)

I don't profess to be an expert in the field of fashion resale. Many second-hand sellers are actually running businesses. If the prospect of earning an income through this avenue piques your interest, I suggest you check out one of the handful of books dedicated entirely to this topic. I'm just an everyday woman trying to monetize my mistakes! The experts, no doubt, have a lot of tricks up their sleeves on how to maximize sales and profit. My purpose here is to offer some basic advice on how to get started on the resale market.

A Picture is Worth a Thousand Words

Take quality photos! Photography isn't one of my greatest skills, but I do make an effort to post attractive and informative images of items I've listed. I make sure to provide photos of all inside tags and labels. I always snap close ups of the fabric, or any special details or flaws that need to be highlighted. Sometimes I'll post a photo of me modelling the garment to provide a better impression of the fit. I usually include the manufacturer's images available online if I can track them down. These professional images tend to display a piece in the most positive light. I also make certain the photos are taken with proper lighting, so the true color of the garment is clearly represented. I have a home with wonderful morning light. Our bedroom makes the perfect makeshift studio for this purpose.

Provide Detailed Descriptions

View your item description as a chance to pitch your sale. Although you may be purging the piece, there was a reason you were drawn to it in the first place. Don't be shy to let potential buyers know what makes the item so special. I try to provide as much information as possible in the description, while remaining honest and transparent. I usually let people know why I'm selling an item, whether it's because it doesn't fit my body or my style. I provide my opinion with respect to sizing. (Does it run big, small or true to size). It isn't in anyone's best interest to try to hide imperfections. I always make sure to highlight any flaws in the garment, and back them up with a photo. If I've made an alternation, I divulge the details surrounding it.

Price Appropriately

When it comes to pricing, you are hoping to recoup as much of your original cost as possible. In most cases, it's unrealistic to expect to recover the full price you paid, even if the tags are still attached. There are exceptions, but generally second-hand goods are sold at a discount.

The easiest way to determine a reasonable price is to research what the same or similar item is selling for elsewhere. Take some time to poke around before you set your price tag.

My advice is to start on the high end of your acceptable range, and lower the price over time if you don't get any bites. Pricing high also gives you room to negotiate with the buyer. (Everyone likes to think they are getting deal!)

Ship Quickly

Once an item sells, make it your mission to ship the parcel as quickly as possible. People love great service, and will appreciate your prompt efforts. They will reward you with five-star ratings, which will only help your selling efforts in the long run.

Deal With Issues Quickly and Professionally

Every now and then you will encounter a dissatisfied customer. If the issue is your fault, I recommend you deal with it promptly and fairly. Everyone makes mistakes, and people are usually very understanding. On the other side of the coin, I know how unrealistic and outlandish some buyers can be. I once had someone accuse me of selling a fake Des Petits Hauts t-shirt (which I had purchased directly from their store in Avignon, France). She wasn't happy with the color (apparently it was the wrong shade of navy), so figured it wasn't authentic. I dealt with the issue immediately. Thankfully I had my original receipt, so the helpful customer service representative at Poshmark shut her down.

STYLISH SECRETS

- Even the most prudent shoppers end up with closet castoffs. We all make the odd fashion mistake! In addition, our wardrobe needs evolve over time as our lifestyles and circumstances change.

- You are better off rehoming your wardrobe rejects than hanging on to them out of guilt. Firstly, someone else will be given the opportunity to enjoy them. Secondly, you can actually recoup some of your financial losses in the process.

- Sending your unwanted items to a consignment shop is a hassle-free solution. Recognize, however, that you will receive only a fraction of the selling price. Consignment fees will eat into your profits!

- It's easier than ever to take responsibility for selling your own goods. There are a number of platforms available that offer great exposure on the resale market. Another option is to set up shop directly on your own social media page!

- When listing an item online, be sure to provide informative and attractive photos.

- Be honest and detailed in your item descriptions. Don't attempt to hide flaws, as this tactic will only lead to a disappointed buyer and a bad review.

- Research a reasonable price based on the current resale value for the same or a similar item. Consider your willingness to negotiate when setting the price.
- Ship sold items as promptly as possible to keep your customers happy.
- Deal with any issues promptly and fairly. Act in ways that will ensure you have a good reputation as a seller.

11

SHOP WITH ME: CASE STUDY

Our time together is almost up! I decided it would be helpful to cap things off with a review of sorts. Would you like to join me on a shopping trip? I thought it would be both fun and informative to have you tag along while I pick up a few additions for my fall/winter wardrobe. I hope I'm not coming across as a geeky accountant, but I figured a good old-fashioned case study would be a great teaching tool!

I'm going to walk you through how I came up with my shopping list, and how I went about hunting down each treasure. Let's get started!

Create a Vision

As I mentioned in chapter 6, my mind is usually a season or two ahead when it comes to wardrobe planning. This means I'm dreaming of fall and winter, just as the first spring crocuses surface from the ground. It's not that

I'm trying to rush my way through the warmer months. I just want to be prepared and organized when fall rolls around. As I've mentioned so many times before, sourcing your wardrobe through preloved avenues requires both planning and patience.

It's time, of course, to pull out my dependable style journal and collect my thoughts. Even though I'm relishing the return of light and warmth, I find myself daydreaming about the cool and crisp days of autumn. I ask myself a series of questions to get the creative juices flowing. What mood and attitude would I like my wardrobe to evoke in the upcoming season? What three words best describe my style? What color scheme am I drawn to? Is there a particular accent color that has caught my imagination? While making notes, I've got my phone open to the Pinterest app. I alternate between jotting down ideas and pinning inspiring images to a board I've labelled "Cold Weather Wardrobe".

My notes and pins reveal that my overall style has remained very consistent since last winter. This is no surprise, as I have spent many years building a wardrobe that suits my personality and lifestyle. The truth is, I adore my cool season wardrobe. I genuinely get excited about the prospect of wearing my jeans, boots, sweaters and heavy woolen coats (of course). After a summer of soft feminine dresses and sandals, I'm always ready to switch things up and tap into the masculine side of my personality. I've always been drawn to menswear-inspired style. My Pinterest board is brimming with dark colors, structured cuts, textured fabrics, military-inspired pieces, lots of denim and leather boots. I plan to stay cozy and warm, and to look good while doing it!

My vision and aesthetic for my upcoming cool weather wardrobe quickly comes into focus. I'm going for a look that is simple, casual and chic (with just a hint of rocker edge). Although I'm perfectly content with what I own, I'd love to add a little spice to the mix. I'll be sticking with my usual color scheme of navy, black and grey, but I've decided it's time to add a splash of color to the pot. My style recipe this season calls for a pinch of red. At this point, I'm still not sure how I plan on incorporating this color into my wardrobe, but I'm excited to see where this style revelation leads me!

Set a Budget

Every January, My husband (also an accountant!) and I set a household budget for the upcoming calendar year. We track our spending throughout the year, so I always know how much I've got remaining in the pot. Before I get too carried away with my master plan, I check in with reality. I pull out my year-to-date clothing budget to assess where things stand. My personal accounting records show that I have $500 left in my style budget. I certainly realize this is a large sum of money for many people. I've gone through periods of life where I would have spent much less. Everyone sits in their own unique financial position, so each one of us is going to have a different number to work with. I am sharing this information strictly for illustrative purposes.

Take Stock

Before I even consider what specific pieces I need or want, my first order of business is to determine exactly what I already have. I usually pick a rainy day to drag my off-season clothes from storage and take stock of what I own. I take this opportunity to examine each piece closely to assess its condition, and whether or not it still suits my style. I may decide to purge a few items. (Selling castoffs is a great way to increase the size of your budget!) I may also decide that it is time to replace certain pieces that are starting to look old, tired and worn. Replacement items are the first entries I place on my wish list.

As I sort through my fall/winter clothing, I make note of two items that need an upgrade. My *black jeans* are getting pretty thin on the knees. I worship these jeans, so I plan to replace them with the exact same pair.

I also note that my *navy-blue cashmere turtleneck* is showing its age. It's been de-fuzzed so many times that it's looking thin and weary! It definitely has a bit of life left in it, but it will obviously need to be replaced soon. Again,

I adore this sweater, so I set my sights on finding an exact replica of it.

Lastly, after months of heavy wear, my two white layering t-shirts are stained, misshapen and ready for the rag bin. I make note to add a couple of *white v-neck t-shirts* to my list.

Create a Shopping List

Now that I have a good grasp on my overall vision, budget and current inventory, I begin to compile my shopping list. I've already got those three replacements pieces on the list. Now I start to consider any new additions I'd like to make. Here's what I come up with based on my overall vision:

- *Black jeans*-replacement piece
- *Navy cashmere turtleneck*-replacement piece
- *White v-neck t-shirts (2)*-replacement piece
- *Denim shirt*-I own a lot of silk blouses, so I like the idea of adding a shirt that is more rugged and durable.
- *Burgundy ankle boots*-I'm going for just a touch of deep red. I decide that footwear is a great avenue to add some subtle color to an outfit. I'd like to find a pair that has an edgy vibe.
- *Navy belt*-This is an item that has been on my wish list for a while. Apparently, navy belts are not that popular,

because I've yet to find the perfect piece. Maybe this season I will get lucky.

- *Pajamas*-I never forget my intimates when wardrobe planning! Underwear and loungewear is always factored into the mix. I'm well covered in the lingerie department, but my loungewear collection is very small. I could really use another set of pajamas to cozy up in during the long Canadian winter.

Map Your Route—Preloved vs New

With my list in hand, I go through each item and come up with a shopping strategy. I don't shop preloved exclusively, so I identify those circumstances I'll be seeking second-hand sources, and those I'll be taking a more traditional approach.

There is one item on this fall's list that stands apart from all the others. I plan to pick up the white tees from Nordstrom. I'm pretty picky in the t-shirt department. It took me forever to source the *perfect* one for me, so I stick with what works. I stock my wardrobe with the Madewell "Whisper Cotton V-neck Pocket Tee" year-round (in both black and white). Most white t-shirts only last a season or two with heavy wear, so I want something that is brand new. They are inexpensive and easy to source online through Nordstrom with free shipping!

I'll be hunting down the remaining items on my list on the preloved fashion market. I'm looking to find high-quality versions of each, so second-hand shopping is a necessity. The retail value of my shopping list far exceeds my budget!

Hunt for Treasure

It's time to get into the nitty gritty details of how and where I hunt down each piece. Let's go shopping!

Black Jeans

These should be pretty easy to track down. I know *exactly* what I'm looking for, since I'm just replacing a worn-out pair from my wardrobe. Because I'm located in Canada, I decide to search the Canadian options first. Shipping is always faster when it is sourced inside our borders, and I know I won't get hit with unexpected duties or taxes.

I begin my hunt on Poshmark, searching specifically for "Citizens of Humanity Rocket". From here I filter the results down to black jeans in my size.

It's my lucky day! I find the exact pair I'm looking for. The seller indicates they were only worn a couple of times and they appear to be in fabulous condition from the photos. They are priced at $55, but I offer $40 for them and she accepts! What a great deal compared to the $250 retail price.

Navy Cashmere Turtleneck

I think I'm in for a challenge with this one. Again, I want to replace an existing piece in my wardrobe with the exact same item—the "Equipment Oscar Cashmere Turtleneck in Peacoat". Sadly, Equipment discontinued this style a few years ago, so they aren't easy to come by.

I check out all my favorite sites with no luck. I'm not giving up hope! I create automatic searches on both eBay and Vestiare Collective for the sweater and cross my fingers that one will pop up soon.

I do spot a black version of the Oscar sweater on eBay that is brand new with the tags still attached. I decide to go ahead and purchase it. These sell for $325 and I pick it up for $100. This is still expensive, but since the style is discontinued, I know I can't go wrong with this classic, timeless wardrobe addition.

White V-Neck T-Shirts

Before buying these from Nordstrom, I take a few minutes to see if I can hunt them down on eBay or Poshmark. I'm only willing to purchase these in brand new condition, and I don't have any luck finding what I want. I pay less than $20 each at Nordstrom.

Denim Shirt

This piece might be tricky to source, as I don't have a specific item in mind! Once again, I decide to begin my search on Poshmark. I recently sold a couple of wardrobe castoffs on this platform, so I have a cash balance available. I love funding new additions this way!

Since I don't have a particular brand or style in mind, I perform a search for "denim shirt" in my size. From here, I filter the results by choosing some of the premium denim brands I'm familiar with. I zone in on something called the "Perfect Denim Shirt" by Current/Elliott. The shirt is listed as size 1. I'm not familiar with this brand's sizing, so I head over to their website and note that this is considered a size small. I request the shoulder, bust and length measurements from the seller, and then compare them to a shirt in my closet. I read online reviews to get a feel for the quality and fit. I offer the seller $30 and she happily accepts! This shirt would normally retail for over $250.

I'm pretty sure this new-to-me shirt is quickly going to become a wardrobe favorite. It's soft, edgy, versatile and fits perfectly!

Burgundy Ankle Boots

I'm a big fan of high-quality footwear, so these boots definitely need to be sourced on the second-hand market. There was no looking back for me when I discovered the

Italian footwear brand Fiorentini+Baker. (Remember how I was inspired by Jennifer Aniston?) I'm determined to track down a pair of burgundy boots that fit both my quality standards *and* my budget!

I suspect it will take some time to track down these boots. Black and brown boots are a dime a dozen, but I've got my heart set on burgundy. After several months, I finally spot a pair on eBay from a seller in Italy. They are new in the box and appear to be a store sample. Since I already own a couple of pairs of Fiorentini+Baker boots, I'm aware that they run very big. I normally take between 7.5 and 8 in shoes, but size 37 (equivalent to a 6.5 or 7 in US sizing) fits me well in their boots. The purchase risk feels low, despite the fact the seller doesn't take returns. (Plus, paying shipping all the way back to Italy would be cost prohibitive.)

I purchase them for $60. I brace myself for a customs bill at the post office, but my boots miraculously slip through some cracks at the border! These retail for around $400. They are awesome boots! I plan to pair them with an edgy all-black ensemble to add that understated splash of red I was looking for.

Navy Belt

Despite my search, I can't find a navy belt I'm in love with. I don't consider it an urgent item, but rather something that would complement my wardrobe nicely. I will continue to poke around the sites for one. I'm confident it will be worth the wait when that special one suddenly appears.

Pajamas

We all deserve to lounge in comfort and style! I've fallen in love with silk pajamas. I actually wore a huge hole in the backside of my last pair. They endured five years of regular wear, so they turned out to be a good investment. They owe me nothing!

I keep a running search on eBay for silk pajamas by Equipment, but they rarely pop up. Silk PJ's by Equipment are really expensive, coming in at over $400. While they aren't worth this price to me, they are worth the wait.

The stars align in my favor, because I receive a notification in my inbox that a pair of Equipment PJ bottoms is available on eBay in my size. Although this is only half of the complete package, I go ahead and purchase them. I've shopped the preloved market long enough to know that the matching top will eventually make an appearance. Sure enough, a couple of months later I'm able to snag the matching shirt on The RealReal. The complete set costs around $80.

These pajamas feel decadently luxurious. I actually enjoy wearing the shirt with jeans on occasion. It is a more versatile wardrobe addition than I expected! Win-Win!

Wool Coat

Are you wondering how a wool coat magically appeared on my shopping list? No, this is not a typo!

I can barely believe my eyes when I spot a tweed Smythe peacoat in my size on The RealReal. I've been lusting for this *exact coat* for over five years ago. Although it's not on this season's shopping list, I don't consider it an impulse purchase. It's been patiently lingering on my wish list, and I realize I need to seize the opportunity and buy it!

It's quite frankly a stunning addition to my wardrobe that I will enjoy for decades. The $75 I pay for it is a far cry from the retail price.

Summary

By inviting you along on my shopping trip, I hope I was able to demonstrate how to put all my stylish secrets into action. You will notice that the outcome of my treasure hunt didn't produce perfect results. I compromised on the color of the sweater, and I have yet to find a navy belt. I also ended up straying from my original plan by picking up a coat unexpectedly. I wasn't overly strict with myself, and chose the easy and convenient option of buying the white t-shirts from a large retailer.

If you are interested in knowing more about the specific items I mention in this case study, and throughout the book, please drop in for a visit on my Instagram account.

I enjoy sharing many of my preloved fashion finds in this space. You can find me at:
https://www.instagram.com/the.elevated.everyday/.

I couldn't resist crunching some numbers at the end of this exercise. I consider these types of calculations a form of good, clean fun (as any accountant would)! The full retail value of my new fall/winter additions totals $2,365. I scooped up everything for $425, which represents 18% of the regular price. I've still got some budget remaining should I stumble across the navy belt or cashmere sweater. I was actually amazed when I compared these totals, as the results were more impressive than I anticipated. It's pretty darn clear, the case for second-hand shopping is compelling!

STYLISH SECRETS

- Spend some time creating a personal style vision and overall wardrobe plan well in advance of each season. Although our tastes tend to remain consistent from one season to the next, it's fun to add a few new twists now and then to freshen things up.

- Give yourself plenty of time to track down the items on your list. Planning a season or two ahead is recommmended.

- Check in with your finances to determine your clothing budget each season.

- Sort through everything you already own to help you evaluate what pieces might be missing from your wardrobe, and whether there are items that need replacing.

- Create a detailed shopping list of the items you would like to add to your wardrobe in the upcoming season. Decide on the best approach to acquiring each piece by determining whether they will be sourced brand new, or through preloved avenues.

- Embark on your treasure hunt. Put all the tips and tricks you learned in this book into action!

A NOTE FROM THE AUTHOR

Thank you so much for reading my book! As a self-published author, I am tremendously grateful to each and every one of my readers.

My hope is that *Preloved Chic* ignited a spark inside you, and has given you the motivation and confidence to jump on the preloved fashion bandwagon. I'm confident the skills and knowledge I've shared will change the way to *think* about and *shop* for your clothes.

As you shift your consumer habits and mindset, you will experience the countless benefits shopping second-hand has to offer. Over time, you will build a beautiful, unique and high-quality wardrobe that suits both your style *and* your budget. Not only that, you will be doing your part to reduce your own environmental footprint. By choosing the preloved route, you will help ensure that garments continue to circulate within the economy, instead of being destined for the landfill.

The resale market is taking the world by storm, and I'm a strong believer that each and every one of us should be trying to participate in this more sustainable form of consumption. I therefore challenge you to pick up where I've left off. Spread the good news! Get your friends and family onboard with adjusting their opinions and shopping habits. I encourage you to share your copy of this book with others, so they too can get in on the action. (Did you know that eBooks can be loaned to a friend for fourteen days through the Kindle platform?) Our combined efforts can have a huge impact on this precious planet. The more people who buy in, the better off we will all be.

If you enjoyed my writing, I invite you to check out my other books—*Elevate the Everyday, Elevate Your Personal Style, Elevate Your Health* and *Elevate Your Life at Home.* They offer a wide range of motivational tips and ideas to bring more joy, comfort, vitality and peace into your life!

I should also mention that I offer a small collection of matching blank journals to accompany all my books. If you are in the market for a pretty new style journal, I have some lovely options available on my Redbubble shop (JenMelville.redbubble.com). I need to add that I'm not trying to shamelessly push branded products on you! I'm a minimalist at heart, and that just isn't my style. I originally created these custom journals as a birthday gift for my mother, but figured it would be fun to open up their availability publicly. Since I enjoy using them myself, I figured others might as well.

Lastly, I have one small favour to ask! I would deeply appreciate it if you would take the time to leave an honest review of this book on Amazon. Not only does this help others discover my work, but it allows me to connect with my readers and gain insight into our shared interests. Over the past couple of years, a number of you have reached out to me, and I've genuinely enjoyed hearing your comments and feedback.

I will leave you now to embark on your very own second-hand fashion journey. Happy hunting!

Much love,

Jennifer

ABOUT THE AUTHOR

J ennifer Melville is a self-published author. She decided to embark on a writing career because she wanted to tap into a community of like-minded individuals who share in her enthusiasm for living well and seeking ways to elevate daily life. She is a professional accountant by trade, who approaches life with an analytical and observant mind. Jennifer has been exploring the concept of elevating the everyday for over twenty years. She is passionate about family, health, fitness, fashion, nutrition, nature and all the beauty life has to offer.

Jennifer lives by the sea in beautiful Nova Scotia, Canada with her husband, two sons and little poodles Coco and Junior.

You can connect with her by email, on her blog, or on her Instagram page.

jenniferlynnmelville@gmail.com

www.theelevatedeveryday.com

www.instagram.com/the.elevated.everyday

Printed in Great Britain
by Amazon

40502638R00081